SECULARITY
AND THE
GOSPEL

SECULARITY
AND THE
GOSPEL

BEING MISSIONARIES
TO OUR CHILDREN

RONALD
ROLHEISER

AUTHOR and EDITOR

A Crossroad Book
The Crossroad Publishing Company
New York

The Crossroad Publishing Company
16 Penn Plaza – 481 Eighth Avenue, Suite 1550
New York, NY 10001

Printed in the United States of America

The text of this book is set in 10/13 Activa.
The display face is Trade Gothic.

Library of Congress Cataloging-in-Publication Data
Rolheiser, Ronald.
    Secularity and the gospel : being missionaries to our children /
Ronald Rolheiser.
        p.   cm.
    Includes bibliographical references and index.
    ISBN-10: 0-8245-2412-8 (alk. paper)
    ISBN-13: 978-0-8245-2412-8
    1. Christianity and culture. 2. Secularization (Theology)
3. Evangelistic work. 4. Missions. 5. Christian education of
children. I. Title.
BR115.C8R65 2006
266′.2 – dc22

                                                                2006006250

1   2   3   4   5   6   7   8   9   10   12   11   10   09   08   07   06

For Wilhelm Steckling, O.M.I.,
Superior General
of the
Missionary Oblates of Mary Immaculate,
under whose leadership and missionary spirit
this project began and flourished

Contents

Part Four
A NOTE ON THE SYMPOSIA AS EVENTS
AND ON OUR KEY RESOURCE PERSONS

PREFACE

T HIS BOOK has a complex origin. Between 2002 and 2004, the Oblates of Mary Immaculate, a congregation of missionaries, worried about how the church is losing ground within secular culture, sponsored four symposia on the topic of how we might be missionaries to our own children, many of whom are no longer walking the path of faith and church with us.

After the last symposia, six of us, Robert Schreiter, Michael Downey, Mary Jo Leddy, Gilles Routhier, Ron Young, and I, met and asked ourselves the question: Given all that was shared at these symposia, what are the key insights we want to share with the world? This book is the result.

Thus, even though I wrote up the synthetic parts of this work, the book has many authors. I'm merely the final redactor, a scribe recording. Many of the ideas expressed in this book were not my own, though I present them confidently and stand behind them. They are the distilled wisdom of many people, professional theologians, priests, religious women and men, pastoral workers, catechists, and laypeople, both old and young. The collective wisdom of a community is often wiser than the best thoughts of an individual. This book is wiser than I am, and I cannot claim credit for much its content. Its content belongs to a community, to the many who participated in our conversations on what it might mean to be a missionary presence inside of our highly secularized cultures.

There are too many people to thank, but I want at least to publicly thank the keynote resource persons who helped direct our conversations at these symposia: Robert Schreiter, John

Shea, Gilles Routhier, Richard Rohr, Mary Jo Leddy, Robert Barron, Michael Downey, Vivian Labrie, John O'Donohue, Tom Rosica, John Allen, Donna Ciangio, Walter Brueggemann, Ron Young, and Reginald Bibby. This is their book as well.

Michael Downey needs special thanks, not just for participating in three of the symposia and contributing a chapter to this book but also for suggesting the concept for the book. Ron Young did countless hours of work in bringing this work to the light of day and needs too to be specially thanked. Finally, I want to thank JoAnne Chrones and Marie Luttrell for their work in editing.

One last point: this is neither a liberal nor a conservative book because what's at issue in the struggle to imagine a more effective way to be missionaries to our own children goes beyond the agendas of both liberals and conservatives. The imagination we are seeking is ultimately found in Jesus. Our struggle is to wake up to it. As one participant put it:

> Jesus offers us a model; he tries to move us from one state to another: we are asleep, and he tries to wake us; we are deaf, and he tries to open our ears; we are dumb, and he tries to open our mouths to speech and praise; we are narrow, and he tries to widen our perspective; we are blind, and he tries to open our eyes; we are lost, and he tries to find us; and we are dead, and he tries to resurrect us. This must be our model within a secularized world.

Ronald Rolheiser

Oblate School of Theology
San Antonio, Texas
November 2, 2005

SECULARITY
AND THE
GOSPEL

PART ONE

Setting the Stage

Chapter One

WALKING THE AMBIT

A Metaphor: The Wide Ambience

I N ANCIENT TIMES, when we still had kings and queens, each year a good ruler was expected to walk around the circumference, the ambit, of his or her kingdom and bring back a report on the state of things. Our notion of a state of the union address takes its origins here. Anthropologically it is called "walking the ambit."

Perhaps that is an apt metaphor with which to begin this book, a "state of the union" report of sorts, on four symposia that the Oblates of Mary Immaculate sponsored on the theme of "Missionaries to Secularity."[1]

The Genesis of These Symposia: The New Mission Field

To understand these symposia, it is helpful to understand their origin and intent. The idea of trying to tackle more explicitly the subject of being missionaries to a secular culture has for us, the Oblates of Mary Immaculate, a double genesis:

More practically, it began at our General Chapter in 1998. During the last days of that meeting, after a new leadership team had been put into place, various regions of the congregation presented key challenges they felt the congregation needed to face during the years ahead. At one point during this exercise, the American region made this observation:

15

We've a proud history as a congregation of going into mission fields in Asia, Africa, Latin America, and the Arctic. However, especially recently, we haven't been nearly as effective within the highly secularized world where, for the most part, people are finding it difficult to pass on their faith to their own children. We seem to know how to be missionaries in faraway places, but not at home. We need to find more effective ways of being missionaries within our culture, the so-called "first world."[2] Today that no doubt is the toughest missionary field of all.[3]

But we did not need a General Chapter to make us aware of this. It is no secret that we, as Christians in the secular world, are having trouble passing the faith on to our own children. Our churches are graying and emptying, and many of our own children are no longer walking the path of faith, at least not public and ecclesial faith, with us. The most difficult mission field in the world today is Western culture, secularity — the board rooms, living rooms, bedrooms, and entertainment rooms within which we and our families live, work, and play.

There is something anomalous about this: all this is happening at a time when there is a spiritual renaissance of sorts happening in the Western world and life at the level of parish and church community has never been more finely tuned, more biblically literate, or more healthy liturgically. We have wonderful programs for nearly everything, a clergy that is well trained, and a laity that is participating more and more in the ministry of the church. For the most part, at the level of parish life at least, we are doing a lot of things right.

The problem is not, it seems, diocesan life or parish structure. We are doing relatively well here. Simply put, for the most part, we know what to do with someone who walks through our church doors, but we do not know how to get people (not least members of our own families) who are not already going to church to enter those doors. We are better at maintaining church life than at initiating it, better at being diocesan ministers than at being missionaries.

What is needed today in the Western world, it would seem, is a new missiology for our own highly secularized culture.

Moreover, the very word "missionary" itself no longer functions effectively within our secularized culture. We automatically link the word "missionary" to sending people to minister in places like Kenya, Burundi, Chad, and Bangladesh, but somehow we cannot form the same kind of concept for sending missionaries to London, Washington, Los Angeles, Paris, or Vancouver. For the most part, we lack the very concept for being missionary in the so-called first world.

What is lacking? What is needed?

We need to become missionaries again within our own culture, among our own children. Secularity is now the culture that, it would appear, the church must most address in terms of taking to heart Jesus' parting challenge: "Go out to all nations and baptize them in the name of the Father, the Son, and the Holy Spirit."

The Intent of These Symposia: Awakening a Missionary Ethos

What precisely were we, the Missionary Oblates of Mary Immaculate, trying to do at these symposia? What, in distinction to the good work that is already being done in missiology departments in various theological and pastoral institutes, did we feel might be our contribution?

As a missionary congregation within which the priority of being close to the poor has shaped and colored our intellectual tradition, we felt that our approach, envisaged as complementary to rather than as critical of other efforts in this area, should reflect precisely what is more unique to our ethos as a congregation sent to minister to the poor.

In terms of a general mission statement, we worded things this way:

This symposium will seek to draw together individuals who in their own preaching and praxis are trying to help create the type of missiology that seeks:

- to go beyond simple maintenance

- to dialogue with secularity in a new way

- to create a new vocabulary for the faith that will speak more convincingly to the present generation

- to discover a more effective way of connecting the gospel to the streets

- to find a common ground between polarized groups within the churches and between the Christian and the secularized world.

Contained in that general intent, however, we wanted these symposia, this particular search for a new missiology, heavily colored by four things:

1. *A concern to develop principles whose fruits were more directed to the rank and file, the poor, and those struggling with their faith and their churches, than to the academy of theology or to the opinion-shapers in the culture.*

Richard Gaillardetz suggests that today we need a new apologetics for the faith, but we need one, he feels, that is not afraid to engage in what might be disparaged as "brute vulgarization" in the service of the needs of the church today:

> Our church desperately needs more theologians who are informed by the best insights in contemporary theology and can present those insights with passion and enthusiasm in ways that affirm and enrich ordinary believers.... We need to encourage theologians not to forsake the church in their legitimate desire to direct the fruits of their scholarship to the academy and society at large.[4]

In essence, that captures one dimension of these symposia. We invited professional academics as experts, but with the intent that their dialogue was to be with missionaries in the field, with pastoral workers in the front lines, with coordinators of diocesan programs, with spiritual directors and people doing retreat ministry, with religious novices and first-level theology students still trying to sort out who they are, with parents who are anxious about their non-practicing children, with questioning individuals who no longer go to church, and with persons who, for whatever reason, nurse various grievances against the church. This made for an interesting mix, one that by its very nature demanded that abstract ideas and principles, however brilliant and valuable in themselves, come down off the podium and be tested practically.

We invited all of our key resource people on the hunch that they were in natural sympathy with just this kind of approach.

2. *A belief that what is most needed right now to inspire us as missionaries within secularity is a re-inflaming of the romantic imagination within religion.*

Good theology stimulates and inflames the intellect. Thomas Aquinas and Bernard Lonergan add that it also helps move the will. The heart needs to have some intellectual vision. Good ideas play no small part in any healthy change.

Thus, the Christian community is always in need of good academics. As history shows, every time the church has compromised on its intellectual tradition, seeing it as unimportant, it has paid a heavy price. Good, sound, abstract, academic theology is perennially the great corrective within church life and spirituality.

More recently we have been blessed with an abundance of good theology. It is hardly the academy of theology that is weak at the present moment. The last thirty to forty years have produced (literally) libraries full of wonderful books on scripture, church history, liturgy, dogmatics, moral theology, spirituality, and pastoral practice. We are not lacking for solid ideas.

What we are lacking, however, is fire, romance, aesthetics, as these pertain to our faith and ecclesial lives. What needs to be inflamed today inside religion is its romantic imagination, and this is not so much the job of the theologian as it is the job of the artist and the saint. We need great artists and great saints, ideally in the same person.

We see this, for instance, in Francis of Assisi. Francis was not a great theologian in terms of academics, and it was not his insights as a theologian that so moved history and transformed Christianity. He does not have major cities named after him and more than three hundred different congregations of men and women trying to live out his charism because of the theology books he wrote. His greatness lay in his art, in his sanctity, and in a particular combination of those within himself. As a great artist and a great saint he was able to inflame the romantic imagination of the church and the world. When he took off his clothes and walked naked out of Assisi, he was not preaching from a pulpit, lecturing from a university podium, or writing a book. He was not an academic. He was an artist and saint who, in that aesthetic gospel gesture, helped restructure the romantic imagination of Christianity and the world in general. Such is the power of great artists and great saints.

We see this too, though to a lesser extent, in the effect of great works of art. For example, the painting of the last supper by Leonardo da Vinci: Today we cannot not picture the last supper as he painted it, even though scholars all agree that Jesus and his disciples at table would not have looked anything like da Vinci's famous imaginative depiction of that scene. But one great artist and one great painting can permanently shape the romantic imagination of the world.

It is this, great gospel art and great saints, that we most need in terms of missiology in the secularized world today.

The theologians are doing their part and, generally speaking, so too are diocesan and parish programs. But solid ideas and solid programs alone are, as we are learning, not enough. We need someone to re-inflame the romantic imagination of Christianity, a new Francis, a new Clare, a new Augustine, a new Thomas More, a new Ignatius, a new Therese of Lisieux.

A re-inflaming of the romantic imagination is too the key to vocations to priesthood and religious life. More than new strategies of recruitment, we need new romantic fire. For example, shortly after he entered the Trappists, Thomas Merton wrote up the story of his conversion and journey to a monastery in a highly idealistic book, *Seven Storey Mountain*. It became a best seller that, among other things, caught the romantic imagination of his generation. For years afterward, Trappist monasteries were flooded with applications, not all for the right reasons, of course, but a large number of men did become good monks because of a romantic ideal that Merton's story triggered.

"All miracles begin with falling in love!" says Morris West. Most lifelong commitments begin in the same way. We need, again, to have a romantic ideal about the vocations of priesthood and religious life; otherwise we can expect still fewer priests, nuns, and religious brothers in the future.

That of course raises the question: What makes for such a romantic ideal? What did Merton's book have that present books on the priesthood and religious life do not have? What works and what does not in terms of firing the romantic imagination?

Mother Teresa's ideal, for example, fires the romantic imagination for some, though not for others. She was a saint, and her ideal of religious life, austere though it may be, is, if anything, wonderfully romantic. But why has it not led to a deluge of young women banging on convent gates in the Western world?

Perhaps more interesting for us in a highly secularized context is the ideal of religious life that is depicted in Sister Helen

Prejean's *Dead Man Walking*. Her story has some key similarities to *Seven Storey Mountain*: both are confessional, are good works of art, make morality attractive, are subtly invitational, show religious life under a good light, are wonderfully romantic, and unearth the hidden monk and nun inside each of us. Both *Seven Storey Mountain* and *Dead Man Walking* make priesthood and religious life a romantic thing. Why has not the latter stirred up the same vocational romance as the former? The task of these symposia is precisely to try to answer such questions.

There are many reasons in the Western world today why our churches are graying and emptying. Conservatives attribute it to the intoxicating power of secularity, to a lost sense of self-sacrifice, to an incapacity in many people to make a lifelong commitment, to the sexual revolution, and to an erosion of faith in the culture. Liberals suggest other reasons: a church out-of-step with the culture, a church too rigid, too hierarchical, too patriarchal, too clerical, too much perceived as anti-life, anti-erotic, anti-world, too much consumed with its own agenda.

There is some truth in all of these reasons, though none is the total culprit. What is? Among other things, we lack a romantic ideal for our faith and church lives. We have too little idealistic fire left. We have subjected faith, religion, and church to a scorching exorcism, and it is now time to move on, to restore to them again their proper angels, their proper light, their beauty. We need to re-romanticize faith, religion, and church and give people something beautiful with which to fall in love.

It was with this in mind too that we chose our periti for the symposia. We had no guarantee, of course, that they were saints, but we had indications from their works that each of them, in his or her own way, was a gospel-artist who could express some of the beauty and romance of faith, religion, and church.[5]

3. *A desire to speak the dialect of the people*

The founder of the Oblates of Mary Immaculate, St. Eugene de Mazenod, was a nobleman, from a background of privilege. As a young man, still quite worldly, not unlike Francis of Assisi, he had a transforming religious experience. Praying before a crucifix on Good Friday, he was shaken to his roots by a realization of God's mercy and God's special love for the poor. This remained within him permanently, a brand in his soul, and he stepped away from his life of privilege to spend the rest of his days trying to serve the poor.

He started the Oblates of Mary Immaculate with that in mind, to serve the poor, and one of the first things he instructed his early followers to do was to learn the language of the poor. Very concretely, at that time in southern France, where he began the Oblate congregation, learning the language of the poor meant learning a hybrid French, a "patois" [dialect] spoken by the servant classes and disdained by the educated and upper classes. To speak "patois" was to publicly mark yourself as poor, uneducated, a domestic, a servant.

The poor suffered more than just a little humiliation for not knowing how to speak the French language properly. Because of this particular poverty they were often left religiously uninstructed and otherwise marginalized. All the preaching and teaching in the churches took place in a version of French that they could not understand. They no longer had access to the gospel. Hence St. Eugene instructed his early missionaries to learn the dialect of the poor and then sent them out to preach popular parish missions in their language.

This trait, to speak the language of the poor, as much as anything else has always marked the charism of the Oblates of Mary Immaculate and has shaped its particular ethos, both intellectually and pastorally. Hence, we wanted that trait too, the language of the poor, to help shape the particular ethos of these symposia.

So we asked: Who has done this effectively today? Who today has learned the dialect of the poor so as to be able to preach the gospel to them in their own language?

What the academy of theology has produced, as we have already stated, is invaluable. Without good theology the community loses its balance. But, with that being admitted, it must be admitted too that for the most part the language of academic theology is not the language of the poor (by any definition of the term). The opposite is often true. The language of academic theology can, unwilling, unwittingly, serve to help deprive the poor of access to the gospel. We all know the jokes and banter about whether Jesus would recognize himself in most theological or scriptural studies written about him. Today, too often, the language of the academy of theology is as inaccessible to the poor (and to most non-professionals in theology) as was the preaching in a foreign language in the churches of southern France at the time of Eugene de Mazenod. Despite all our sincerity and good will, too often in our teaching and preaching we have not learned to speak the dialect of the poor. We are, too much, preaching the gospel in a foreign language.

This, we believe, is particularly true inside secular culture. The language of secularity and the language of the gospel have become foreign tongues to each other.

There are some exceptions of course, and one of those exceptions that we chose to highlight as a model for the symposia was Henri Nouwen, perhaps the most renowned spiritual writer of our time. What made Nouwen so popular (and he is one of the most read spiritual writer in the English language in both Roman Catholic and Protestant circles) was not just his depth, though that was unique; it was also his language. He, more than most others, had mastered the patois of the poor.

Nouwen used to rewrite his books many times over in an attempt to make them simpler and simpler, to make them accessible to more and more people, independent of their background and education. In doing that, slowly through the years, he developed his own language, a certain language of the heart, a language of the poor, and a language of faith for secularity.[6]

There is a certain formula to that language that can perhaps serve as a paradigm for the rest of us. Nouwen might be the closest thing to a "missionary to secularity" that our generation has produced, and his attention to language, to the dialect of the poor and the language of secularity, was not incidental. It was highly intentional. Examining the elements of his language we can extrapolate a certain formula. That formula suggests that an effective vocabulary for the faith within secular culture includes learning a certain "patois" of the poor and walking a certain tightrope. Our language needs to be:

- radically simple — without being simplistic

- carrying deep sentiment — without being sentimental

- self-revealing — without being exhibitionist

- deeply personal — yet profoundly universal

- clearly Christian — but not the inner-table-talk of the worshiping congregation or the rote repetition of biblical language and metaphor

- devotional — without being pious

- clearly committed, speaking from a defined place — yet never hard, judgmental, exclusive, or doctrinaire

- contemporary — without being full of cliché, fad, hype, and "cool"

- highly moral — without the alienating rhetoric of political correctness

- invitational — yet respecting freedom and not proselytizing

- iconoclastic — yet always respecting where people are in their development

- deconstructionist — yet always offering the tools with which to build

- the language of critical thought — yet ever the positive aesthetic of the gospel-artist

- a language that radiates the joy of the resurrection — even as it leads ever deeper into the paschal mystery

- the language of soul — yet ever the language of spirit

- the language of energy — but as initiated by wisdom, full of color and tempered by gray

- a language deeply sensitive to human weakness — even as it challenges that weakness and invites to what is more sublime

- the language of compassion — yet never compensatory

Among other things, these symposia were an attempt to look at the question of language: What vocabulary for the faith do we need today to speak to the secular world in general and to the poor in particular? Nouwen's language was presented as potential paradigm.

4. *A particular view of secularity*

Finally, we wanted these symposia too to take a particular view of secularity.

Too common within religious circles is the view that secularity is the enemy, that it is anti-church, anti-Christian, amoral, and the root of most of our religious problems. The antithesis of religiosity, it is assumed, is secularity.

In planning these symposia, we chose to take a different view of secularity, seeing it, not as the enemy of our faith tradition, but as largely our own child, the adolescent offspring of our faith tradition, historical Judeo-Christianity.[7]

Seen in this light, it becomes understandable that secularity will often be belligerent, angry with us, accusatory, full of adolescent grandiosity, and occasionally downright hostile.

That is not uncommon behavior of children toward their parents. But your own children are never your enemy, even when they are hostile.

Have you ever watched a typical, moody adolescent interact with his or her family in public? Picture a sixteen-year-old girl in a restaurant with her parents and younger siblings. She is at the far edges of both the table and the conversation, ashamed of her family. It is obvious that she is simply enduring her family with less than subtle patience. Her speech, manner, body language, almost everything about her suggests disaffection. Yet we know enough to not take her attitude all that seriously. It is common and natural. When you are sixteen, your family can do nothing right, you are ashamed of its faults, and your parents and siblings seem the prime agents blocking your freedom, potential, and growth.

That, we believe, is an apt image to describe how so many people within secular culture, wanting to be mature and sophisticated, relate to our Judeo-Christian roots and the churches. Nurtured in a culture that was born largely out of a Judeo-Christian womb, many stand at the edges of their religious heritage, hypercritical about the religious family they have been born into, and convinced that their Christian roots are what stand between them and proper freedom, achievement, and enjoyment. Whether it is expressed or not, this is the spirit that undergirds much of the anti-Christian, anti-ecclesial, and anti-clerical feeling within our time.

This metaphor, taken from the writings of Kathleen Norris, captures more than what is evident at first glance.[8] What it suggests is that in both a hypercritical young person and in the attitude of many of us today toward our religious roots there is a lot of adolescent grandiosity, but that this is natural and something that is generally outgrown. A lively, struggling, iconoclastic adolescent, hypercritical of her family, is not bad, just unfinished. She only needs to grow up more to come to appreciate who and what gave her the freedom, tools, and self-confidence to stand on her own and be critical.

Louis Dupré, the renowned philosopher at Yale University, says the same thing, though in academic language. Answering the question, "Should modernism be reversed?" Dupré replies:

> I think not. Instead, we ought to return to, and elaborate, the fundamental principle of modernity as it was first enunciated half a millennium ago: human creativity must and can be developed in full integration with the transcendent and cosmic components of the ontotheological synthesis. Contrary to current anti-modernist theses I consider the program of modernity not obsolete or in principle wrongheaded, but unfinished.[9]

The intellectual disaffection with Christianity today is not bad. It is just unfinished. It needs to grow up more and become cognizant and appreciative of the fact that the heritage that it has been so critical of is the very thing that has given it the freedom, insight, and self-confidence to speak all those words of criticism. It can learn something from the young man or woman who at thirty-something, now carrying real responsibility, begins more and more to appreciate and drink from the wellsprings of his or her family heritage, despite seeing the family's faults. We see this all the time: the bitter, distrustful adolescent, mouthing criticism of the family from the edges, growing into the responsible adult at the center, grateful for how the family has shaped his or her soul.

A Catholic feminist was once asked: "How can you be a Christian theologian and a feminist? Are these two not incompatible?" Her answer: Christianity helped give us feminism! The historical roots of feminism and of almost everything else in the Enlightenment, which takes as non-negotiable the values of individual freedom, democracy, equality of opportunity, and respect for others, lie largely in the Judeo-Christian scriptures. It is no accident that these values have arisen so strongly out of Western Judeo-Christian culture. It has simply taken us a long time to understand more deeply the demands of our own heritage.

Alfred North Whitehead suggests the same is true for science and technology.[10] The road for their development too was paved by the Judeo-Christian scriptures. It is also no accident that science and technology emerged in the West. In the end, despite current protests to the contrary, it was Judeo-Christianity that gave us the Enlightenment and its making sacred of the values of individuality, equality, democracy, tolerance, and rationality. But, like an adolescent feeling her oats, the Enlightenment, right into our own time and culture, believes that it has been its own source of wisdom, self-taught, a child without parents.

Gil Baillie likes to say: We didn't stop burning witches because we stopped reading scripture; we stopped burning witches because we kept reading scripture.[11]

A haughty adolescent girl is not bad; she's just unfinished. That is also true for the Enlightenment and so much of what it has spawned, including secularity and the anti-Christian and anti-ecclesial spirit of our time.

We convened these symposia with a certain preconception of secularity. Its negative underside notwithstanding, we viewed it not so much as our enemy, but as our child, with its opposite being not the church but the Taliban. The participants in our conversations, however, as we shall see in the next chapter, had their own views.

Notes

1. The first symposium took place at St. Paul University in Ottawa, June 20–22, 2002; the second at the Oblate School of Theology in San Antonio, October 3–5, 2002; the third took place again at the Oblate School of Theology in San Antonio, Texas, October 21–23, 2004; and the last, a much smaller gathering, took place in Toronto, April 15–16, 2005.

2. We acknowledge the difficulty associated with the term "first world." Among other things, there is an implied superiority in saying "first world" in counterdistinction to "second world" or "third world"; there is, as well, the naive, unconscious assertion that the highly secularized world, "the West" (a term which is itself problematic), is a center from which other places must take their reference. As David Tracy puts it: "We, in North America and Western Europe, retain the secret wish that we are still the center and can name those others. The others remain at the margins. Marginal from where? From the center which no longer holds. In theological studies, this naming continues, for example, when we not so innocently refer to 'Near Eastern' and 'Far Eastern' studies; near to whom? Far from what? The other envisaged from a self-named center is too often a projected other . . . [and] . . . even with all the talk of otherness and difference — there is no longer a center with margins. There are many centers" (David Tracy, *On Naming the Present* [Maryknoll, NY: Orbis Books, 1994], 4).

With all of that being admitted, however, we will still, with full acknowledgment of some of the unfortunate baggage the term is carrying, occasionally use the term "first world" simply because, for our readers, it makes things clear much more quickly.

3. The extended statement to the General Chapter fleshes this out even more: "Concerning mission in secular and de-christianized areas. The simple reality is that most of the first-world countries today, countries that were considered Christian countries before, are themselves mission countries. This is so first of all because of huge numbers of impoverished immigrants as well as massive numbers of middle-class people who have simply stopped believing the gospel of Jesus Christ. There is a strong feeling that we need leadership from the General Administration in the profound appreciation of this fact and the implications this has for our missionary reality. . . . We would like some high octane thought put into developing a sense of mission that goes deeper than just a geographical sense of mission, i.e., just sending missionaries to places we haven't been to before. Some of the energy and enthusiasm that we see dedicated to opening missions in new places needs also to be directed to re-focus and re-energize the work of living the gospel in places where it has withered. Not to do so will further add to the insensitivity of the first world towards the needs of the masses of impoverished in the world" (*Acts of the Thirty-Third General Chapter of the Missionary Oblates of Mary Immaculate* [Rome, 1998]).

4. Richard Gaillardetz, "Do We Need a New(er) Apologetics," *America* (February 2, 2004): 30. Gaillardetz goes on to add that whenever professional theologians ignore the pew for the academy, invariably somebody with a more simplistic agenda steps in and, in a much less healthy way, takes over that role: "As long as theologians are content to lecture only in university classrooms and limit their publications to scholarly pieces in academic journals, the theological community will continue to cede the stage to those who offer a narrower and more rigid appropriation of the Catholic tradition and are willing to bring Catholic theological heritage to the people and provide them with the substantive 'meat' for which they yearn" (ibid.).

Cambridge professor Nicholas Lash would agree. What's needed in adult religious education today? A happier marriage between the academy of theology and the church pew, Sunday school, the diocesan newspaper, and all catechesis in general: "We need to bring the resources of a mature and literate Christian imagination to bear upon the circumstances and the issues of people's daily lives" (*Tablet*, April 15, 2000, 514).

Daniel Berrigan, in a harsher moment, is less positive about this marriage ever taking place. The theology of the academy, he submits, has too little interest in such a marriage: "It is rare to find, in theology departments for example, that scripture or a given religious code, is considered binding, or a call to faith. Theology, like every other discipline, is often considered an object of competence, not of faith; dry grist for the mill. Religious traditions, which have historically nourished heroes and saints, are treated as matters of 'specialty,' 'expertise.' Their outcome in a given instance is nothing like a unitive conscience, political sense or passion, wisdom. None of these. But a small-minded, cold-fish attitude toward the world" (Daniel Berrigan, *Poetry, Drama, Prose*, ed. Michael True [Maryknoll, NY: Orbis Books, 1991]).

5. Cardinal Francis George has a different formulation of this. In trying to describe what Andrew Greeley is attempting in his novels, he comments: "He [Greeley] is trying to re-evangelize the imagination of the culture."

6. At first glance, one might well dispute this: Did Henri Nouwen really speak the dialect of the poor? Didn't he rather speak, just more effectively than most others, precisely the language of the middle and upper classes, the educated, the yuppies?

That's true, but there's paradox hidden inside it. It's precisely in the area of having a vocabulary for the faith where the middle and upper classes inside secularity, the yuppies, are impoverished. The preaching of the gospel is often as inaccessible to them, in terms of language, as it was to the poor in Eugene de Mazenod's time. They're hearing it in a foreign language. They share this precise impoverishment with the poor and, in this, they too are the poor.

Nouwen's writings may well have been written with more than the socioeconomic poor in mind, but he did, very much, have the poor in mind: Like Eugene de Mazenod he deliberately "stepped down" from a certain privileged state. In Nouwen's case this meant a "stepping down" from academia, from intellectual sophistication, from anything that could complicate the language of the faith so as to render it, for whatever reason, inaccessible to the non-professional, the non-intellectual, the non-privileged. One sees this "stepping down" from privilege in Nouwen's life as a whole. He left prestigious professorships at Harvard, Yale, and Notre Dame to live in L'Arche, a community founded by Jean Vanier to live and work with the mentally challenged.

And it's interesting to observe how Nouwen developed in terms of language during the nearly thirty years he wrote in English. Right from the beginning, from this first books written from Notre Dame in the early 1970s, he had an itch to word things as simply as possible, but, being a psychologist by background, a lot of psychological terminology filtered through. More and more, however, through the years, one sees a certain purging of that and, more and more, one sees a language that simply speaks to the heart (e.g., his book *The Return of the Prodigal Son*).

You see similar efforts at language within the work of Richard Rohr, Kathleen Norris, John Shea, Robert Barron, Jim Wallis, Mary Jo Leddy, and Daniel Berrigan, among others. Thomas Moore and James Hillman, although they do not speak out of an explicit or committed faith stance, are very helpful in that they are helping us clarify what constitutes a "language of soul."

7. Admittedly, secularity was not spawned by Judeo-Christianity alone, but by a certain marriage of this tradition with the Greco-Roman tradition. The child of this marriage, Western civilization, which so strongly includes secularity, bears wonderful qualities from both parents: Clearly we can see the parenting of the Greco-Roman side in the place it gives to rationality, logic, and law; indeed the very principle that undergirds modernism and secularity (i.e., that critical reason should be the final arbiter of all truth, the real priesthood in the culture) comes largely from the Greco-Roman parent. On the other hand, much of its moral principle comes from the

Judeo-Christian parent and is today so much taken for granted, wedded to rationality, and understood as somehow self-evident, that it's no longer admitted that its DNA is religious, Judeo-Christian in this case.

8. Kathleen Norris, *Amazing Grace: A Vocabulary of Faith* (New York: Riverhead Books, 1998).

9. Louis Dupré, "The Dialectic of Faith and Atheism in the Eighteenth Century," in *Finding God in All Things: Essays in Honor of Michael Buckley*, ed. Michael Hines and Stephen Pope (New York: Crossroad, 1996), 51.

10. Alfred North Whitehead, *Science in the Modern World* (New York: Macmillan, 1925).

11. Gil Baillie in a private conversation. See his *Violence Unveiled* (New York: Crossroad, 1995).

PART TWO

The Fruits of
Our Conversations

Chapter Two

SECULARITY AND
ITS MANY FACES

Secularity: A Mixed Bag

N OT EVERYONE reacts the same way to the word "secularity." For some, it connotes most everything that is a good: freedom, equality, human dignity, rationality, democracy, the movement beyond irrational fear and superstition, the possibility of science, the opposite of fundamentalism, and an opening of the human mind and spirit that should, appropriately, be spoken of as an "enlightenment." For them, secularity helped end the dark ages, the burning of witches, the Inquisition, and the feudal world with its system of unfair privilege and narrow religious intolerance. In this view, secularity is more friend than enemy, and it is a major moral achievement, bought at a considerable price, that should not naively be taken for granted, nor challenged too uncritically in the name of God and religion.

For others, while not necessarily denying that it brings some positive things, secularity connotes more darkness than light. In this view, secularity also means godlessness, the loss of faith, the weakening of divine and church authority, sexual irresponsibility, excessive individuality that ultimately undercuts community, the breakdown of family life, the depreciation of the church's contribution to civilization, and, as Pope Benedict XVI sometimes puts it, "the dictatorship of relativism." For them, secularity is more an enemy than a friend and is a force to be challenged in the name of God and religion.

Who is right? Or, perhaps more accurately, how much truth lies in each view?

As the opening chapter of this book confesses, these symposia were convened with the hunch that, while secularity clearly does bring elements that need to be challenged in the name of God and religion, it is still, of itself, a moral achievement and is more friend than enemy to God and the church. The antithesis of secularity, it was asserted, is not the church, but the Taliban.

However, our conversations also questioned that view, even strongly at times. Where did we eventually land? Was there a consensus view? What ultimately, after four separate symposia, would we like to say about secularity?

After all of our conversations, what we want to share on the notion of secularity itself might be summarized in four points:

1. *Secularity is a complex phenomenon, and that complexity needs to be respected.*

Secularity is not monolithic. It has taken on, and continues to take on, very different historical expressions. There is not just one kind of secularity.

Moreover, secularity also has complex relationship to the world as a whole. We commonly use the expression "our secular world," but in fact secularity, in the bigger global picture, is itself an island in a sea of faith, and an island that is today under attack from fundamentalists of all kinds within that sea of faith.

There are, as well, major pockets of non-secularity inside of secularity, and, as we will see later in this chapter, there are various generations within secularity.

Yet, with all of this being said, secularity does admit of a certain common definition, at least philosophically. How might one define secularity?

More simply it can be defined, as many dictionaries do, in this way: Secularity is a term coined (c.1850) to denote a system which sought to order and interpret life on principles taken solely from this world, without recourse to belief in God and a future world. Given this background, the term today more generally designates the tendency to ignore, if not to deny, the principles of supernatural religion.[1] Thus we speak of the process of secularization when, for instance, we see a government agency taking over an institution (for example, a hospital, an orphanage, or a university) that was formerly run by a church. In moving from religious hands to non-religious hands, that institution is now considered to be a secular one.

While this defines secularity, in caption, a fuller definition can be also be useful: Scholars in the history of Western philosophy commonly divide that history into four major eras: the *ancient*, covering all the years until St. Augustine, 354–430; the *medieval*, covering the years from Augustine until René Descartes, 1596–1650; the *modern*, covering the years from Descartes (often dubbed "the father of modernism") until the mid-twentieth century; and the *post-modern*, covering the years since. Secularity can, in essence, be identified with the third era, *modernity*.

What is modernity?

Philosophically, modernity takes its origins in René Descartes and can defined in this way: To be modern is to believe that *human reason should be the final arbiter for how we ultimately structure common life and the final authority on how we should govern all public life*. Modernity asserts that human reason is the ultimate authority. Descartes ushered that principle into Western thought, and we see its radical character only when we compare it to what went before — and what still exists almost everywhere else.

Prior to modernity, the final governing principle for Western culture, and virtually every other culture, was not rationality, but divine authority. Prior to modernity, what trumped everything else was a statement of divine authority: "God says! The Bible says! The church says! The king or queen says!" In a modern framework that argument no longer works, as we know. Instead the ultimate arbiter is: "Reason says! Democracy says! Rationality says! Agreed-upon principles say!" Secularity arises out of this.

Secularity is more than just the process of secularization, with more and more areas of life and more and more institutions shifting from church to non-church control. Ultimately, it is a question of authority, namely, what is to be the final authority in terms of organizing and controlling public life? Divine authority (God, the Bible, the churches) or human reason (reason, the democratic process, a rationally agreed upon course of action)? Secularity believes that it is the latter. That, in essence, defines secularity.

But that ideal definition has taken on different historical constellations, particularly in terms of what place is given to God, faith, and the church. Sometimes, for instance, as in the French Enlightenment, secularity has shown itself more hostile to religion. Sometimes, however, as in the case of the Scottish Enlightenment (which deeply influenced how church and state are separated in the United States), it was less hostile. Today, too, individual secular cultures vary in terms of their attitude toward God, faith, and church. Concrete secular societies, as one symposium member put it, are always "a hybrid of configurations of secularism and religion. One shape doesn't fit all." Secularity has a variety of faces.

Moreover, secularity is an evolving reality and, as it changes, so too do its attitudes toward God, faith, and the church. Thus, concretely, within our various secular cultures we see that attitudes toward religion run the gamut from hostility ("The sooner the churches are eliminated, the better!") to intellectual condescension ("These poor folks still actually believe in another world!"), to indifference ("God, faith, and the church are a non-factor!"), to a positive, vital relationship that looks to God, faith, and church to be key players in the search for wholeness, peace, and security in a post–September 11, post-modern, and post-secure world ("Today we need God, faith, and the churches more than ever!").

We recognized the complexity of secularity, and the first major point our symposia would like to make is that this complexity must be respected. To treat secularity, without highlighting and respecting its complexity, is to lay a bad foundation for any conversations between it and the Gospels.

2. *Secularity is also mixed, morally and religiously, and that too must be respected.*

Secularity is, our symposia concluded, multivalent. And that multivalence carries a confusing moral ambivalence.[2]

Secularity should not quickly be demonized or divinized. It is neither simply "a culture of death," nor is it simply "a culture of life." Morally, it is ambivalent. It is full of grace, even as it is full of many things that make grace, faith, and a full moral life more difficult.

As suggested in the opening chapter of this book, secularity not only has many deep moral strengths, it is in its genesis the child of Judeo-Christianity, and its deep structure incarnates many of the moral strengths one finds inside the Judeo-Christian tradition.

Sometimes its critics forget that, while secularity mandates freedom from religion, it also mandates freedom for religion, and its moral strengths run deep, even if those moral qualities are no longer attributed by many secularists to any religious source. Simply stated, secular culture, with some inconsistencies notwithstanding, contains much of what is best morally in the Judeo-Christian tradition: human dignity, fundamental honesty, concern for others, democracy, equal voice for everyone, equality of race and gender, equal opportunity for all, tolerance of others and their differences, sexual responsibility, solutions for conflict that do not involve violence and war, hospitality, decency, courtesy, fairness, and an openness to God and the transcendent. It also contains an energy and a color that, as Soviet Marxism (which, while brutally secular itself, had in effect outlawed color) discovered, is vital to sustaining a healthy life.[3] Faith and church must be very nuanced in their challenge of secularity.

Critics of course are quick to point out that secular culture does not always demonstrate these moral qualities. True, but Christianity does not always demonstrate its ideals either. A culture, like a religion, needs to be judged by its more noble expressions, not by what is deviant from its ideal. What is most noble within secularity, not unlike Christianity itself, has not been tried and found wanting, but has, like the ideal of Christianity, been found difficult and seldom fully tried. Secular culture, in its ideal, purports many of the deep moral values that are rooted in the Judeo-Christian tradition and, at times, has even played a major role in re-teaching those ideals to the churches.

But its critics are right when they point to certain moral inadequacies as well. Rationality, independent of faith, does not always play God very well. Secular culture does, in fact, struggle with a certain "dictatorship of relativism." This manifests itself, among other ways, in an excessive individualism that is often at odds with the common good, in a certain adolescent grandiosity toward God and church, in financial economies that often work mainly to the benefit of the rich, in sexual irresponsibility, in the failure to properly value and support the family, in abortion, in euthanasia, in pornography, in drug abuse, in the vulgarization of parts of the entertainment industry, and a diminished sense that humanity needs both divine protection and divine guidance.

Our symposia concluded that secularity is morally a mixed reality, neither fully angel nor fully demon, but, at one and the same time, full of both grace and sin. As people of faith, we need to appreciate its many moral strengths, the protection it gives us for our faith, and the historical fact that it is more our child than our enemy. Conversely, we must challenge its moral inadequacies, particularly its own religious grandiosity, that is, its belief that there is no God outside of itself.

3. *We are invited to have a certain biblical and Catholic attitude toward secularity, namely, to love the world as God loves it.*

Where did our symposia ultimately land in terms of suggesting an ideal attitude toward secularity? Again, despite differences, a certain common thread of ideas emerged.

We underscored the point made by the Oblate General Chapter of 1998 in the opening section of its final document, "Evangelizing the Poor at the Dawn of the Third Millennium," where a challenge is laid out: "If God continues to believe in women and men, how can we despair of them?"[4] If God loves the world, should we not love it too?

But what is implied in our loving the secular world? Our symposia would like to highlight four interpenetrating aspects of that love:

(a) We are asked to love the world, even with its moral inadequacies and in its sometimes hostile attitude toward faith and the religion.

Biblically, we see that God loves us not because we merit that love and are free of sin and fault. Rather God loves us because God is love and cannot not love. God loves us in spite of our sin. As Jesus says: "God lets his sun shine on the bad as well as the good." Like the sun, which does not discriminate between the vegetables and the weeds, God's love shines on all and on everything, independent of moral merit.

Our attitude toward secularity must mirror that. We are called by our faith to love the world (and that includes the very flawed cultures we live in), not because it is everywhere good and deserves our love, but because God is love, non-discriminatory love, and our belief in God asks us to incarnate that non-discriminatory love in this world.

Secularity, we assert, is not an enemy to be fought, but a child to be loved.

(b) We are asked to be *in* the world, but not *of* the world.

A clear imperative that comes to us from the incarnation itself (where God takes on human flesh) and is ratified strongly in the thrust of Vatican II is the principle: be in the world, but not of the world.

It is easy, as we know, to fall off either side of this tightrope: We can be other than the world, but not in solidarity with it; or we can be so immersed in it and so identified with it that we no longer bring it anything that is transcendent to it.

Our symposia recognized both dangers, but placed its challenge more in the direction or risking being in the world, not perhaps so much in terms of calling us away from the sanctuary, rectory, convent, seminary, prayer-group, or religious dress, but in terms of first being in solidarity with the pains, hopes, fears, and joys of our world, before moving on to challenge that world from the point of view of the gospel and the cross.

This, we recognize, demands a new maturity, a new inner-directedness, that is strong enough to immerse itself in the world without losing its moral and spiritual salt because it is rooted solidly enough in something and Someone outside the world.

Our challenge to the secular world must not be framed in a duality that sets us against the world. This is not just religiously false, it is also fundamentally dishonest, a denial of reality. We must recognize that we ourselves are part of this world, of secular culture, not outsiders who stand untainted at some anthropological and moral distance. We are children of this world and are inextricably bound up in our culture. We too easily protest how bad our world is and how evil is modernism, even as we write those criticisms up on a computer ("modernism-in-a-box"), communicate on the Internet, step off airplanes, enjoy modern medicine, and especially enjoy the religious protection that secular society gives us. Ultimately, if we are honest, we need to acknowledge that there are no categories of "them" and "us," as if being men and women of faith somehow no longer makes us part of the human family. There is only the one valid category, "we," humanity, the world, all of us together, one family, inside a common search.

We are part of the human family and are ourselves part of secular culture, for good and for bad. Our engagement with secularity must acknowledge this fact, assume that there is good will and sincerity in the world, and not fall into any kind of oversimplistic duality within which we see ourselves as good and the world as evil.

(c) We need to be careful so that in challenging secularity we do not find ourselves "fighting against God."

All good things come from God. There is only one author of all goodness. Jesus makes that point clearly.

There are, as we all admit, many good things, good moral things, within secularity. The fact that secularity does not attribute its origins to God does not negate the truth that all good things come from God.

We must therefore be very careful, very qualified, and very nuanced in our challenges to secularity. If we challenge it simplistically, without first recognizing and blessing what is good within it and exempting that goodness from our critique, we will end up not following the wise counsel of Gamaliel in scripture, where he tells a sincere but overzealous Sanhedrin to be careful in what they challenge because they could easily find themselves "fighting against God" (Acts 5:39). Gamaliel would have found himself at home at these symposia.

(d) We need to root our critique of secularity in the classical Catholic principle that the world is flawed, but not corrupt.

During one of the symposia, a keynote speaker suggested that we need to confront "the pathology of secularity." That prompted a series of strong objections, concluding with a certain consensus that, while there are pathologies within secularity, of itself, secularity is not a pathology. And, just as there is sin in the world, the world itself is not to be identified with sin.

Catholic anthropology, we recognized, in partial counter-distinction to the classical Protestant reformers, has always asserted that the world is flawed by sin, original and other, but is not fundamentally corrupted by it. Our engagement with secularity must be grounded in this truth; the world is flawed but not evil.

In summary, the secular world is not a moral cesspool within which faith's primary task is to convert the godless. The secular world is still a world loved by God and a world with much moral and spiritual strength. In the name of faith, we are called to love that world.

We recognized too that, given the principle that we respond to challenge most deeply when we recognize that the one challenging us first loves us, the secular world will respond to us precisely, and only, when it first recognizes and feels our love.

Finally, like *Gaudium et Spes*, we recognized that we are also being evangelized by the culture, even as we are evangelizing it. We are, as the Vatican II document says, benefiting as a church from many things within the culture, including even from the opposition and occasional hostility of our world.[5]

4. *Secularity is a non-negotiable given, our milieu, and we live in hope, knowing that the Gospels are up to the task of engaging secularity.*

Our symposia concluded that the positive and negative features of secularity, both together in all the ambiguity that that radiates, constitute the milieu and the horizon for our evangelizing efforts. They are the missionary field today.

Our faith, moreover, gives us confidence that the Gospels are more than adequate to the task of engaging secularity.

Again and again, indeed in virtually every theophany in scripture, the first words that the divine messenger addresses to us are: "Do not be afraid! Be at peace!" Those are an important missionary instruction. We must engage secularity without fear, confident that our truth, our Gospels, and our God are up to the task. Too often there is an unconscious fear that our scriptures, church, and God are not up to the task and that they must be protected from the secular world. That fear masks a lack of hope. The Gospels still work!

The Gospels are not so much beautiful deposits of truth that must be protected, but seeds to be thrown into the world, and, at times, in imitation of the Sower sowing the seed, even thrown rather indiscriminately. And they must be thrown in hope and confidence, knowing that the seeds are up to the task.

"God," as one keynote speaker put it, "is not in trouble if people in a secular world stop going to church! God, in fact, is never in trouble at all!"[6] In our engagement with secularity we must radiate that deep truth. God does not need to be protected, even when the world naively thinks it is bigger than God.

The choice today is not so much between faith and secularity as between faith and cynicism. Jim Wallis, the founder of *Sojourners* and perhaps the closest thing our generation has produced to a Dorothy Day, puts it this way:

> Prophetic faith does not see the primary battle as the struggle between belief and secularism. It understands that the real battle, the big struggle of our times, is the fundamental choice between cynicism and hope. The prophets always begin in judgment, in a social critique of the status quo, but they end in hope — that these realities can and will be changed. The choice between cynicism and hope is ultimately a spiritual choice, one that has enormous political consequences.[7]

Secularity: Various Generations
Sharing the Same Time in History

Karl Rahner once quipped that we should never take for granted that everyone who is alive at the same time is part of the same generation.

That is a very insightful comment and sheds light on another aspect of secularity, namely, individuals and groups relate to secularity in very different ways in terms of faith and religion.

We see this, first of all, in the fact that within all secular cultures there are major pockets and communities of religious fervor. This is often seen in immigrant communities where God, faith, and religion often still play an important role in life at all levels. But it is not limited just to immigrant communities (and the implicit, simplistic assumption that someday too they will secularize).

Secular cultures show an increasing differentiation within themselves, namely, different groups of people are beginning to relate themselves quite differently to the modernist principle that reason is to be the final authority on the planet. For example, some individuals and groups who, while still solidly committed to most of the basic principles of secularity, are now beginning to describe themselves as being post-modern, post-sophisticated, and post-liberal. Some commentators, looking at this, speak of a "second modernity," of a new secularity that recognizes the positive values within classical modernism, but now sees the need for new boundaries and for some authority beyond pure reason, beyond precisely the "dictatorship of relativism."[8]

Moreover, sociologists of religion have pointed out that, while church attendance in all secular cultures has decreased rather sharply, God and the churches have a greater staying power than a simplistic reading of secularity suggests. The vast majority of people within most secular cultures still believe in God, and the vast majority too still claim some religious affiliation, even if most no longer go to church regularly. The crisis (if one should even use that word) is much more ecclesial than religious. What is suffering most is church life, not belief in God.[9]

Moreover, secularity is differentiated in still another way, namely, there are (in a manner of speaking) different generations within the same generation.[10] What does this mean? A picture is worth a thousand words: Imagine almost any church congregation on a Sunday morning. The minister or priest presiding is not facing an ecclesial, ideological, emotional, or political homogeneity. Rather he or she is looking at three or four different ecclesiologies right within the same congregation and is looking, as Robert Schreiter might say, at "two-and-a-half separate ecclesial generations."[11] Not everyone in a church pew thinks and feels the same way.

This has, we recognized, important implications for evangelization and mission. Among other things, it complicates the question: "What do people want today?" There is, it seems, no stereotypical secularized man or woman or stereotypical secularized Christian. People relate very differently to secularity and consequently often look for very different things from their faith and their churches.

We see some of this playing out in a certain new "generation gap" developing inside many churches. In many churches today we are witnessing an increasing ideological and ecclesial tension building as a younger generation (to put the matter simplistically) is moving much more toward a theological, ecclesial, and liturgical conservatism.

That there are different generations within the same generation today is obvious — and the tension is unpleasant. On the one hand, a more liberal generation is looking at this and seeing in it a pathology, an unhealthy quest for security, even as a more conservative generation is seeing the liberalizing movements in theology and the churches during the past thirty or forty years as a certain sellout of the gospel and an accommodation to the world.[12]

The symposia debated the pros and cons of the growing proclivity for conservatism in the churches and recognized that this is an important phenomenon that begs us to "read the signs of the times" with courage. It heard the voices of young Christians who, in speaking of their religious background, described feeling like "they were picking up the pieces of a shipwreck." These same young voices spoke too of their desire for substance, for wholeness, and for more public display within the living out of the faith, pointing to happenings like the World Youth Days as events that deeply energized them religiously.

The symposia also recognized the importance of a certain new "volunteerism" among many youth, the desire of many youth, within all denominations, to give themselves in some form of service, often in an international setting, for a number of years. Indeed one symposia participant posed the question: "Might serving in an NGO [Non-Governmental Agency] be a new form of religious life?"

We had no full answers to these questions or to the present tensions within our churches, but we recognized that these questions and tensions point to a very important fact that should be highlighted and respected: secularity has various generations within itself, and all missiological engagement with secularity must respect that fact.

Secularity:
A Time of Ecclesial Diminishment

"A symptom suffers most when it doesn't know where it belongs."[13] A certain ecclesial diminishment within secularity is indeed a symptom that, too often, does not know where it belongs.

Our symposia accepted the fact that, within secular culture, there is a clear and, at places, even a radical ecclesial diminishment. This is not a good time for the churches. This is seen not just in plummeting church attendance, but also in the ever increasing marginalization of religion and the churches in terms of public life. This marginalization is often characterized by an indifferent attitude toward the faith and churches and a lesser respect for the churches' voice in moral issues such as war and abortion, but sometimes too it takes a more hostile expression in anti-clericalism and in anti-church and anti-Christian attitudes.

Within secular culture, the churches no longer walk triumphant, and their voice is often no longer seen as the moral high ground. Far from being in a culture of clerical and ecclesial privilege, we now live in a culture of clerical and ecclesial disprivilege. This has been heightened in North America and Western Europe, particularly in the United States, by sexual abuse scandals among some clergy and church organizations. These scandals have become a symbolic lightning rod around which much anti-clerical, anti-ecclesial, and anti-institutional anger has constellated. The churches, for their part, feel not just humbled, but also humiliated.

How do we "read the signs of the times" in this diminishment? Where is the finger of God in all of this?

Our symposia chose to read this in a biblical fashion. God is pruning us. We are undergoing a collective, ecclesial dark night of the soul. Dark nights of the soul, as we know, can be triggered by one of two sources: infidelity and sin on our part, or God's withdrawal of former consolations in function of pruning us. In either case, its meaning is the same; we are being called to deeper conversion.

Various biblical metaphors were suggested in terms of trying to see our present ecclesial diminishment through the prism of faith. Biblically, we saw ourselves as being "in exile" and "in the desert." Exile and the desert are places too. Indeed they are biblical places, places of hope. Once they have done their work in us, we will be the better for it.

Irrespective of the specific metaphor, the feeling was that we are being purified, cleansed, pruned in our faith and that, as painful as this is, is a necessary thing. As one participant put it: "The church was never meant to be so powerful and strong, an 'Empire' itself. In our diminishment we are meant to learn not just humility but especially reconciliation and forgiveness." Another put it this way: "This diminishment is trying to teach us that we need to leave something, abandon certain securities, and let God lead us in a new way."

Looking at the new situation that faith and the church find themselves within secularity, we identified with the early Christians, the church of the Acts of the Apostles, where the early followers of Christ had to learn what it meant to be church, to create church, and to evangelize, without having prefabricated models with which to work. The church's new place inside of secularity has many parallels to this.

A final metaphor offered to help read our present situation apposite to our ecclesial diminishment within secularity was the story of Abraham and Sarah, who got pregnant in late life, beyond when it should have been biologically possible to do so. As one participant put it: "As our churches age and get more gray, perhaps, like Abraham and Sarah, we can have a gray-haired pregnancy!" That, no doubt, captures some of the missionary task for our aging, graying churches within secularity.

Secularity:
The Need for a Kenotic Christology

In his keynote address at the symposium at St. Paul University, Ottawa, Michael Downey posed this question: How do we speak of God inside a culture that is pathologically distracted, distrusts religious language and church institutions, and yet carries its own moral energy and virtue?[14]

That is an important question when so many of our own children, siblings, and friends no longer go to church and are challenging our religious beliefs. They certainly fit Downey's description: distracted, distrustful of religious language and church institutions, yet carrying a lot of moral energy in their

own way. In terms of evangelization and missiology, what do
we do in the light of this?

Among other things, Downey suggested that we need an
image of God and of Jesus that shows what God does in these
situations. What image of Jesus might be helpful here?

There are, as we know, many images of Christ, both in
scripture and in our church traditions. Christ is presented
variously as shepherd, king, teacher, miracle-worker, healer,
bread of life, sacrificial lamb, lover, among other images. Different ages have tended, for their own reasons, to pick up
more on one of these than the others. What might be a fruitful image of Christ for our culture, one within which so many
of our own children no longer walk the path of explicit faith
with us?

Downey made a suggestion that was very much endorsed
by the symposia participants. What image of Christ might be
most helpful today in terms of missiology and evangelization?
The image of Christ as the kenosis of God; Jesus as divine self-
abandonment; God as emptying himself in the incarnation.
What does this mean?

In essence it is captured in the famous early Christian
hymn quoted in St. Paul's letter to the Philippians:

> Make your own the mind of Christ Jesus:
> Who, being in the form of God,
> did not count equality with God
> something to be grasped.
> But he emptied himself,
> taking the form of a slave,
> becoming as human beings are;
> and being in every way
> like a human being,
> he was humbler yet,
> even to accepting death,
> death on a cross. (Phil. 2:5–8)

What this text and many other parts of Christian scriptures tell us is that, in Christ, God offers a love so pure,
so self-effacing, so understanding of our weaknesses, so self-
sacrificing, and so "self-emptying," that it is offered without
any demand, however veiled, that it be recognized, met, and
reciprocated in kind. In the incarnation, God, like a good
mother or father, is more concerned that his children are
steered in the right direction than that he, himself, be explicitly recognized and acknowledged for who he is and thanked
for it. God, like any parent, takes a huge risk in having
children. To have children is to leave yourself painfully vulnerable. It is also to be called upon for an understanding, a
patience, and a self-dethroning that, literally, can empty you
of self. That is as true of God as of any mother or father.[15]

When a mother or father sits down at table with the family,
she or he does not need, want, nor expect, to be the center of
attention, a prerogative a healthy adult generally cedes to the
children. What the parents do need and want is that the family
be happy, respect each other, respect the ethos and aesthetics
that the family values, and that all the family members are
essentially on the right track in their life and know what is
ultimately sacred, moral, and important, even if given members do not, at this particular moment, recognize or credit the
family for what they have been given to prepare them for life
and happiness.

This is even truer of God, whose love, understanding, and
patience are beyond our own and who, like any good parent,
does not demand to be always the center of our conscious
attention.

We need, our symposia believe, a theology of God and
an image of Christ that can give us both vision and hope
as we engage secularity. That theology of God and image of
Christ, we believe, very much in line with Downey's suggestion, should take as its horizon God's "self-emptying" in Jesus
Christ.

What are the qualities of this "self-emptying"?

To "self-empty" in the way Jesus is described as doing means being present without demanding that your presence be recognized and its importance acknowledged; it means giving without demanding that your generosity be reciprocated; it means being invitational rather than threatening, healthily solicitous rather than coercive; it means being vulnerable and helpless, unable to protect yourself against the pain of being taken for granted or rejected; it means living in a great patience that does not demand intervention, divine or human, when things do not unfold according to your will; it means letting God be God and others be themselves without either having to submit to your wishes or your timetable.

There is, as scripture tells us, a time for everything. That is also true for how proud or humble we are in our evangelizing efforts. Hence, a time of exile, a time of pruning, a time of ecclesial diminishment, a time when faith and the churches are being marginalized by the culture, a time of ecclesial disprivilege, a time of being humbled by sexual abuse scandals, and a time when many of those nearest to us no longer walk the path of explicit faith and church with us is too, we feel, a time to anchor ourselves in the crucified wisdom of the God-man who emptied himself out of love.

This too, we felt, needs qualification. Grounding ourselves in Christ's kenosis as God's modality of presence in the world can also be a simple rationalization for our present ecclesial diminishment and an excuse for lack of religious commitment and fervor. Is this not simply a way of exempting ourselves (as many conservative critics would challenge) from taking a scathingly honest look at ourselves and how our immersion in secularity has weakened our courage to speak out in faith? One might also legitimately ask whether the exact opposite is not true, namely, is it not precisely when we are down and humbled that we should be proclaiming most loudly and explicitly the fact that God is triumphant and still in charge?

There is some substance to both of these critiques: Looking at what is happening to explicit faith and church life within secular culture and simply writing it off as "God's kenosis" (and a very healthy development) is, we agreed, far too simplistic. This certainly was not what Downey suggested. As several keynote addresses, particularly those of Robert Barron and Thomas Rosica, pointed out, perhaps today more than ever we need to shed our fear and have the courage to proclaim our faith publicly and even with pageantry.[16]

However, with that being admitted (and added in as a challenge), we still felt that, given the situation of faith and the church today within secular culture, "reading the signs of the times" asks that we see a finger of God in our ecclesial diminishment. A triumphalistic church is being pruned and, all our objections to the contrary, we are in fact being ever more marginalized and humbled inside the culture. There are many ways to read this, but we chose to read it biblically: God's finger is in this, and that finger, experienced in a present ecclesial kenosis, is directing us to let go of certain triumphal forms of power so as to take our place again among the poor and humble.

Notes

1. See, for example, *The Concise Dictionary of the Christian Church*, ed. E. A. Livingstone (Toronto: Oxford University Press, 1977), 467.

2. David Tracy, in an essay that demonstrates both his remarkable scholarship and insight, highlights both the moral strengths and weaknesses of secularity. See *On Naming the Present* (Maryknoll, NY: Orbis Books, 1994), 3–24.

Our symposia also highlighted three features within secularity that we need to take more seriously in our engagement and dialogue with it: (1) its quest for meaning, (2) its distrust of institutions, and (3) its concern for the environment.

3. Doris Lessing once stated that she left the Communist Party because "it didn't believe in color."

4. This document is available from the General Administration of the Oblates of Mary Immaculate, CP 9061, 00100 Roma-Aurelio, Rome, Italy. E-mail: *gensec@omigen.org*.

5. Vatican II, *Gaudium et Spes,* article 44. The translation of the text in Austin Flannery's 1981 edition reads this way: "Whoever contributes to the development of the community of mankind on the level of family, culture, economic and social life, and national and international politics, according to the plan of God, is also contributing in no small way to the community of the Church insofar as it depends on things outside itself. The Church itself also recognizes that it has benefited and is still benefiting from the opposition of its enemies and persecutors" (*Vatican Council II, The Conciliar and Post-Conciliar Documents,* ed. Austin Flannery [New York: Costello Publishing Company, 1981], 947).

6. Reginald Bibby, in his keynote address given at a symposium in St. Albert, AB, June 18, 2004.

7. Jim Wallis, *God's Politics: Why the Right Gets It Wrong and the Left Doesn't Get It* (San Francisco: HarperSanFranciso, 2005), 346. Wallis then goes on to make this comment about the temptation to cynicism: "First, let's be fair to the cynics. Cynicism is the place of retreat for the smart, critical, dissenting, and formerly idealistic people who are now trying to protect themselves. They are not naive. They tend to see things as they are, they know what is wrong, and they are generally opposed to what they see. These are not the people who view the world through rose-colored glasses, the ones who tend to trust authority or who decide to live in denial. They know what is going on, and at one point, they might even have tried for a time to change it. But they didn't succeed; things got worse, and they got weary. Their activism, and the commitments and hopes that implied, made them feel vulnerable. So they retreated to cynicism as the refuge from commitment."

8. See Robert Schreiter's essay, chapter 5 of this book.

9. See, for example, the works of Reginald Bibby, Canada's foremost sociologist of religion. An essay of his appears later in this book (chapter 10). Bibby is fond of quipping that even the churches have greater staying power than is commonly thought. People haven't left their churches, he often says, they just aren't going to them! One of the reasons for this, he submits, is that today, at least in the secularized cultures of the West, people are treating their churches much like they are treating their families. So contact is on their own terms and at their own convenience and is most wanted at special occasions and around rites of passage. It's public life and family life that are in trouble, and ecclesial life is an extension of that.

10. See Robert Schreiter's essay, chapter 5 of this book.

11. Ibid.

12. One of the perceptions at the symposia was that, while secularity is spiritually hungry, it is also often rather illiterate in terms of its reading of the place of community and ecclesiology within spirituality.

13. James Hillman, *The Force of Character* (New York: Random House, 1999), 129.

14. See Michael Downey's essay, chapter 6 of this book.

15. One of our keynote speakers at the Ottawa symposium, Vivian Labrie, interpreted this concept, God's kenosis, in a more radical way, at least in her phrasing of it. God, she submits, "is mature enough so that he doesn't demand always to be the center of our conscious attention." At one point in her presentation she fantasized how God can give people permission to "take a vacation" from God, but only after God says this: "I give you a vacation, including permission to not have to talk about me. But I have a suggestion. Do something useful on this vacation, that is, work for the poor, try to narrow the gap between the rich and the poor, and in doing so you might find new perspectives on heavenly issues." Labrie's presentation, which was given in French and was not presented as a formal paper, is not reproduced in this book.

16. See Robert Barron's essay, chapter 9 in this book. Thomas Rosica's presentation, which was oral and not in the form of a formal paper, is not recorded here.

Chapter Three

MISSION TO AND WITHIN SECULARITY

Being Missionaries within a Secular Culture

W HAT IS OUR MISSION to and within secularity? How do we become missionaries to our own children?

As outlined in previous chapters, our symposia tried to describe and define the *soil* of secularity. How receptive and how resistant is it to the word of God?

We suggested that secularity as a potential soil for faith and church is both complex and ambivalent. It is a soil that is receptive and resistant both at the same time. We suggested too that it is not our enemy, but our child, the child of the Judeo-Christian tradition. But it is not yet full-grown, mature enough to fully understand and appreciate what it has drawn from its parents. Too often we see this manifest in a certain adolescent grandiosity, in an arrogant and hostile attitude toward its own roots. However, as is the case with any adolescent child, this is quite understandable, even if unpleasant.

Finally, and perhaps most important, we affirmed our belief that the gospel is adequate to the task. God and the gospel do not need to be protected; they stand up to everything, even secularity. Our mission to secularity, we suggested, must therefore be grounded in hope, risk, and openness rather than cynicism, fear, and intolerance. The great, non-discriminating Sower, God, is still throwing the seed into the world, and the secular world is soil of all kinds — rocky and resistant, shallow and choked with weeds, but also fertile and good.

   With this as a background, we suggest the following principles in trying to be missionaries to and within secularity.

   1. *Our mission to and within secularity needs to be non-proselytizing and non-combative, a mission within which we see ourselves as walking with our own children who, while they have much to teach us, desperately still need our support, moral guidance, and constant cajoling.*

If we believe this metaphor is accurate, namely, that secularity is not our enemy but our child, and if (as Louis Dupré and Kathleen Norris) suggest, that child is "not bad, but just unfinished,"[1] we then need to extrapolate some lessons from this metaphor as to how we should approach secular culture as we try to live out Jesus' mandate that we baptize all nations in the name of the Father, and the Son, and the Holy Spirit.[2]

   How do loving, concerned parents interact with their own nearly full-grown children when those children question or ignore the family's values, are excessively absorbed in their own lives, or are actively hostile toward some of the family's cherished beliefs and ways of doing things? Especially how do those parents interact when those same near-adults are often full of an enviable energy and zest that their parents often lack and when their criticism of the family sometimes contains deep truths that expose some long-standing inconsistencies and hypocrisies within the family?

   There is no normative, detailed script for this, as all parents know, but there are some general principles. The most essential one is that parents continue to love and support their children, in spite of differences and tensions. Love does not withdraw at the first sign of disagreement and tension, or at the first sign of hostility. However, to love others is not necessarily to agree with them or support those areas of their lives that are at odds with our own moral and religious sensibilities. Good parents continue to love, even as they continue to challenge and even as they refuse to compromise their own beliefs and cherished traditions. Good parents love their children but stand their moral ground without compromise. Good parents too admit that they need to listen to the challenges that come from their near-adult children, even as they challenge in return.

Good parents too know that to love and effectively challenge an adolescent who is nearing maturity means walking a painful tightrope between saying too much and saying too little, between challenging and nagging, between being supportive and compromising, between sustaining a connection and losing it, and between being a respected moral voice and being written off has having nothing to say. A missiology that is concerned with speaking to and within secularity has much to learn from this.

Our mission to secularity must therefore be non-combative. It may never see secularity as its enemy or even as a territory to be conquered. Rather, images of accompaniment, familial exchange, mutual challenge and comfort, helping to bring a near-adult (our own child) to a fuller maturity, and strong challenge (especially by our own refusal to make moral compromise) are, we suggest, more helpful.[3]

2. *Our mission to and within secularity must be in solidarity with the poor, the vulnerable, the powerless.*

"Nobody gets to heaven without a letter of reference from the poor!"[4] That is also true for effective mission. Nobody evangelizes effectively without taking seriously the non-negotiable scriptural imperative that our faith is judged by the quality of justice in the land, and that is itself to be judged by how the most vulnerable groups ("widows, orphans, and strangers") are faring.

Again and again our conversations reminded us that mission and evangelization are not just about private morality and our private lives but also about God's preferential option for the poor and God's mandate that we actively work to create peace and justice. Part of evangelization is also the movement to eliminate poverty and injustice.

Beyond this general though very important principle, what else did our symposia suggest here?

First, that the poor, and only the poor, can supply us with a certain type of wisdom, namely, the wisdom of the crucified, the wisdom of the one who is actually enduring the cross. The poor must help give us our eyesight. Thus we must be more deliberately attentive to where we live and to whom we listen because where we live and to whom we listen will largely determine what we see. We must always be sure that we are linked to the poor in such a way that we see their reality and hear their voice.

Second, part of our mission within secularity is to help articulate both the different modalities of power and the different modalities of powerlessness. Not all power is bad, just as not all powerlessness helps open one to God and the gospel.

Power too can be beautiful and a service to the gospel. Everywhere (in politics, in the church, on school playgrounds where bullies rule, in neighborhoods torn apart by drug dealers, and in the world at large where private interests often destroy community) there is a longing and a constant prayer for someone to come and use power in a redeeming way to make things better. The longing for a messiah is in fact a longing for a redeeming power to enter into our lives.

Our history is full of examples not just of the misuse of power but also of the sacred and moral use of power. For example, the founder of the Oblates of Mary Immaculate, St. Eugene de Mazenod, was born into privilege, but he stepped down from that to be with the poor and to serve them. The same holds true for many men and women of generosity and faith, including a spiritual giant of our own time, Jean Vanier, the founder of L'Arche. Their stepping down from wealth and privilege becomes a beautiful form of power that helps the poor. We are called to imitate this stepping down, a movement which itself imitates what Christ did when he emptied himself and took on the form of a slave (Phil. 2:6–8).

However, even that, we acknowledged, virtuous as it is, is itself a luxury not given to the poor and runs the risk, if not properly understood, of falsely idealizing poverty and power-lessness. Poverty is not beautiful and can, just like riches, corrupt the soul. As one participant put it: "Power corrupts, but so too does powerlessness."[5]

Mission to and within secularity calls upon us to step down from privilege to be more in solidarity with the poor and powerless, even as we never idealize or glamorize poverty.

3. *Our mission to and within secularity needs to witness particularly to fidelity and stability in a culture too much given to infidelity and instability.*

One participant, a missionary among the Native peoples in Canada, shared that whenever he arrives in a new mission invariably the first question asked is, "How long do you plan to stay with us?" Before he is questioned about his message, he is questioned about his fidelity and his long-term commitment.

That simple example speaks volumes. Stability and fidelity are clearly not the strengths of secularity. High transience is forever tearing up our roots, and our proclivity to constantly reinvent ourselves is creating a climate within which it is easy not to trust anything or anybody long range. We have become used to everything shifting, to cherished truths being debunked, to neighbors moving away, to governments breaking promises, to people not keeping their word, and to relationships to which we vowed lifetime fidelity dissolving.

However, as we noted at these symposia, despite all of this, the heart and spirit still ring true. At the end of the day, almost everyone still wants real roots, words they can trust, permanent relationships, fidelity in commitments, weddings in white, truths that are eternal.

Our mission to secularity, we feel, must be particularly prophetic in how it highlights and incarnates fidelity, trustworthiness, and rootedness. This, we acknowledge, will be not so much a question of saying the right words as of being in our own lives witnesses of fidelity and trust. As one participant put it: "We could use a saint at a time like this!" Sanctity, in the secular world, is very much linked to fidelity.

4. *Our mission to and within secularity needs to incarnate a fuller maturity, a new inner-directedness, and a wider inclusivity.*

Karl Rahner once stated that today within Western culture the time is approaching where one will either be a mystic or a non-believer.

Among other things, what he is saying is that within secularity today men and women of faith are no longer the cognitive majority. Instead, everyday consciousness is now essentially agnostic. The majority of people still believe in God, but as Nietzsche pointed out a hundred years ago consciousness of God is dead in market squares and in the places where we recreate and live our ordinary lives.[6] And, he predicted, given this death of God in the ordinary consciousness, eventually consciousness of God will disappear within the churches as well.

Partly, Nietzsche has been proven right. Today, by and large, our communities no longer carry the faith for us. Often this is true too of our own families and closest friends. We often find ourselves very alone in our faith, in a moral diaspora, feeling religiously and morally lonely, unanimity-minus-one. This is true even in our churches where we can too easily experience "religion without God."[7]

To have a vibrant faith today requires (as Rahner puts it) a certain mysticism. Sociologists might term this more crassly as a "cognitive deviance." Within secularity, the everyday communities we live and work in are less and less helpful to us in terms of supporting our faith. Hence, there is a new imperative and a new burden in terms of sustaining faith: we either carry it ourselves, through deep, personal conviction, or we do not carry it at all, at least not in any vital sense. This situation, our symposia recognized, asks of us a new maturity, a new inner-directedness, and a new missiology.

What, more specifically, are the implications of this for evangelization and mission?

At the Synod of the Americas, held in Rome in 1997, the Canadian bishops, in an intervention on the topic of immigrant Catholicism in Canada, made the following statement: "In Canada we know how to be Catholic when we are poor, under-educated, and culturally marginalized; but we do not know as well how to be Catholic when we are affluent, educated, and accepted in the cultural mainstream."[8]

In essence, that describes one of the major missionary tasks inside of secularity. Up until recently, our missionary efforts worked well, but they worked well (and continue to work well) among a certain group of people, namely, the poor, those outside the cultural mainstream, and those who are still within strong communities. When this sociology breaks down, so too does church attendance. We face, as the Canadian bishops clearly put it, a new task today. We need to model in our lives how one can be affluent, highly educated, cultur ally inside the mainstream, and struggling with the excessive individuality within secular culture, and still be a man or woman of faith who is deeply committed inside an ecclesial community.

For many of us, perhaps most of us, this is a new task. In a manner of speaking, we are pioneers because we are entering into a new territory without many previous models to guide us.

Pioneers often have to struggle in their new countries. Our symposia recognized that it is easier to diagnose this problem than to fix it. We humbly admit that we are not, at this stage, in any way close to writing up anything in the way of a practical pastoral program for missionaries to secularity. We are willing however to suggest some important directions and general orientations.

Since many of secularity's struggles with faith and church stem from its overfixation on modernity, individuality, affluence, sophistication, and liberality, our efforts to evangelize within this culture call upon us to, in our message and our persons, to move toward being more post-modern, post-individual, post-affluent, post-sophisticated, and post-liberal. Paul Ricoeur's term, "second naiveté," perhaps best describes what is being asked of us.

But this must be distinguished from something that looks similar but is in fact very different, namely, a new conservatism that is "anti-modern" and "anti-liberal," but names itself "post-modern" and "post-liberal." To become post-modern, post-liberal, post-affluent, and post-sophisticated requires, first of all, a journey through modernity, liberality, affluence, and sophistication that appreciates their strengths as well as their weaknesses. Simply put for the sake of clarity, one is never post-affluent if one has never been affluent. We must first have something before we can outgrow it.

"Anti-modernism" and "post-modernism" might look the same at first glance, but looks are deceiving. In the former case, the underlying attitude is that modernism is a bad thing which must be opposed, whereas in the latter case, the underlying attitude is that modernism, like adolescence, is a good thing, but something we move on from as we grow. "Second naiveté" should not be confused with the innate innocence of a child, just as childlikeness should not be confused with childishness.

Effective missionaries to and within secularity must help show secularity how it can grow to a new maturity by moving beyond where it is at present in terms of its overfixation on modernity, affluence, and sophistication, but this must be envisaged not as a return to a former conservatism but as growth to something new, a post-modernity, a post-affluence, and a post-sophistication.

How is this to be done?

Again, our answers were humble and focused more on general directions than on practical programs. Where is this new maturity to be found? We suggest that, as men and women of faith concerned with being missionaries to our own children, we need to develop more fully two capacities:

♦ *The capacity to walk a finer tightrope in the mandate to be in the world but not of the world.*

"Be in the world, but not of the world!" Great advice, but never easy to do. We struggle to live out this tension without giving in falsely to one side or the other.

The temptation on the one side is to keep ourselves pure and unstained from contamination from what is bad in the world, but at the cost of excessively separating ourselves from the world, not loving the world, not leaving ourselves vulnerable as Jesus did, and not modeling for the world how someone can live inside the world and still be a man or woman with a vibrant faith and ecclesial life. The other temptation, of course, is the opposite: we enter into the world, love and bless its energy, but do so in a way that ultimately offers nothing in the way of being salt and light for the world. We simply melt into secularity and become part of it.

We recognized that our struggles here are sometimes the result of bad theology: too often we have neither a proper theology nor a spirituality to guide and sustain us in this, nor do we have sufficient personal or collective maturity to walk this tightrope.

What kind of theology and spirituality can help us? What kind of personal and collective maturity is asked of us?

What is asked for is a theological vision that helps us hold, in proper tension, our love for the world and our love for God.[9] One may not be sacrificed for the other, but they must be brought into proper relationship.

Hence we need a theology and a spirituality that create for us a vision within which we are able to love the world and bless and honor its goodness, its energy, its color, its zest, and its innate moral strengths, even as we stand where the cross of Jesus is forever being erected and speak prophetic words of challenge in the face of the world's moral deficiencies and injustices, its self-preoccupation, its proclivity to greed, and its reductionist vision. In this vision of things, the latter should never be done without the former. Unless we first honor and bless what is good in our world, we do not have the moral right to criticize it. Worse still, if we do not honor the world's energies and color we will not be honoring God who is the sole author of all that is good — including the world's energy and color.

In essence, we need to be in solidarity with our world in everything but sin, blessing it with one hand, even as we hold the cross of Christ (and the judgment it brings) with the other.

But that, as we acknowledged, is not easy. Simply put, too often we lack the moral and emotional strength to imitate Jesus, who could walk with sinners, eat with them, forgive their sins, feel the pain and chaos that sin creates, embrace everyone, be present in the world, bless and enjoy its good energies, and yet not sin himself.

This is not an abstract thing, but an earthy one: too often we cannot live as Jesus did simply because we lack the maturity to walk amid the many temptations, distractions, and comforts offered us by our world, without, on the one hand, losing ourselves in them, selling out our message, or, on the other hand, unhealthily protecting ourselves by withdrawing into safe enclaves to huddle in fear with our own kind, protected from the world, but at the cost of denigrating its goodness, energy, color, and zest and being less than fully alive ourselves.

It is no accident, one participant pointed out, that our ecclesial communities sometimes look fearful, gray, sexless, and uninviting when compared to the freedom, color, eros, and energy that is manifest in the world. Our problem sometimes is that we remain religious, but at the cost of also being fearful, timid, frigid, and depressed. It is hard to be an effective evangelizer when one is either depressed or perceived as being depressed.

What is being asked for is, perhaps, expressed well in this comment, made by a participant in the discussion on vocations and the renewal of religious life:

> What we'd need today is a religious community which would have no rules, because none would be needed. Everyone would be mature enough to live out a poverty, chastity, and obedience that would not need to be overly protected by restrictive rules and symbols that set one apart. Attitudes and behavior would rather be shaped from within, from strong convictions coming from a mature heart and from a commitment to a community, a vision, and a God that puts one under a deep voluntary obedience. The community would be mixed, men and women living together, but those within it would be strong enough to affectively love each other, remain chaste, and model friendship and communal living beyond sex (and without denigrating sex). The community would live an unsheltered life, be radically immersed in the world, and its members, sustained by prayer to God and community with each other, would be free, like Jesus, of curfews and laws, to dine with everyone, saints and sinners alike, without sinning themselves. This community would give itself to the world, but resist being of the world.

Perhaps that is a naive fantasy. It would require a community of saints. But the reaction to this fantasy spoke volumes. Everywhere there was the spoken and unspoken question: How can I find that? Show it to me and I will join tomorrow!

What we realized is that the missiology and evangelization are predicated on much more than pastoral strategy and technique. To be more effective missionaries to and within secularity we must, like Jesus, have the personal maturity to walk inside our world and be present to both its grace and its sin, even as we remain sinless ourselves. Like the three young men in the book of Daniel, we must be able to walk right into the fire, without ourselves being consumed by it because we are singing sacred songs inside the heart of the fire (Dan. 3:19–30).

• *The capacity to have a wide, catholic, ecclesial embrace*

Beyond the need for a new maturity in our personal lives, we felt that being missionaries to and within secularity calls for a new ecclesial maturity as well. What is being particularly asked of us today, we felt, was a wider, more universal, more catholic, ecclesial embrace.[10]

In a world and a culture characterized by division, bitterness, historical hurt, intoxicating ideologies, and growing intolerance, what kind of ecclesial community do we need in order to be a light to the nations? Where, ecclesially, can we give a witness that is particularly salt and light for the secular world?

We suggest that where we need to be salt and light in today's world is especially in our inclusivity, in the width of our embrace as an ecclesial community. We need to incarnate more of what Jesus taught when he said, "In my Father's house there are many rooms" (John 14:3).

In saying this, Jesus was not commenting on celestial architecture, but on scope of God's heart. In God's heart there are many rooms. Sadly that is not always the case in our churches.

One of the apostolic marks of the church is that it is *catholic*. In this context, "catholic" is not to be understood in opposition to "Protestant." Rather the term here means wide, universal, nonsectarian, all-inclusive, beyond narrow boundaries, the opposite of all intolerance. What is opposite to catholicism is not Protestantism, but fundamentalism. In a fundamentalist's house there is only one room.

Our conversations recognized that today, everywhere in the world, within secular cultures and outside of them, we are witnessing the growth of new fundamentalism, new intolerance, new exclusivities, and new ideological divisions. The important ecclesial challenge in this is that of building a church community that is wide enough to embrace the divisions, the ideologies, the old historical hurts, and the new wounds. What is being asked of us, we submit, is to build a church beyond our personal theologies, personal tastes, personal agendas, private ego, private grandiosity, historical hurts, and personal wounds. This wider inclusivity also includes the challenge to build a church that is post-ideological, beyond liberal and conservative, beyond the right and the left, and even beyond the middle.[11]

"Sing to the Lord a new song!" When we pray that invocation in the context of our search for a more effective missiology, we might well ask ourselves the question, "What was our old song?" What is missing in what we are presently doing?

What can we do that is new? Haven't we already tried almost everything imaginable? What stone have we left unturned? There are, after all, only so many ways of doing ministry, of trying to preach, of reaching out to those who do not come to church with us. What more can we do?

We can have a wider ecclesial embrace, respect more people and more things, and we can hold more polarities in proper tension. This, in our present ecclesial and cultural context, would be new. Perhaps an example might help clarify what is meant here.

As these symposia were being planned, the Oblates of Mary Immaculate also launched a new mission, a pilot project, to try to incarnate these principles within a concrete missionary endeavor inside of a highly secularized setting.

Four young Oblate missionaries, three priests and one brother, were chosen and sent to Birmingham, England, to found a new mission, taking as their setting the Bullring shopping district, one of the largest shopping plazas in the world.[12] As part of their preparation for this mission, they spent some months together in reflection and retreat, pondering, among other things, what they might offer that is unique. While doing this, they looked at a number of efforts that were already being made to be more deliberately missionaries within secularity.

What they saw were a number of very commendable projects, which each in its own way had a certain success. But all too often a given project, despite its goodness, effort, and sincerity, would also have a particular ecclesiology, ethos, and ideology that would make for a certain exclusivity in its embrace.

For example, some projects focused on the sacraments and devotions and drew in a good number of people, even young people. A lot of their activity happened inside churches, in shrines, at pilgrimages, at World Youth Days. The approach here was very traditional, as was the dress of the missionaries (clerical collars, soutanes, liturgical vestments). The appeal was to the mainstream, and the invitation was to make yourself solidly at home inside the institutional church.

Some of the other projects took a very different, almost antithetical, approach. There was no focus on sacraments and prayer at all, except in rare instances. The missionary venue was not a church or a shrine or a pilgrimage, but a secular setting, a bar, a hostel, a coffeehouse, a drug-laden street corner, and the dress of the missionaries was not clerical but casual — blue jeans, cut-offs, T-shirts. The appeal was not to the mainstream but to those on the edges, and the invitation was not so much to make yourself solidly at home in the institutional church but rather to a prophetic presence at its edges.

Looking at all of this, the missionary team at Birmingham asked themselves, "Why not both? Why not both sacraments and bars, clerical collars and blue jeans, justice and devotions, the prophetic edge and the institutional church, attention to the margins and to the mainstream? Why not all of these things inside the same missionary team and missionary approach?" To bring all of these diverse elements, each part of a truly Catholic ecclesiology, together into one community, they felt, would be what is new. It would also, they believe, capture the imagination of those many people who find that, too often, they have to make false choices between churches and bars, blue jeans and clerical dress, justice and the devotional life, the institutional and the prophetic. To sing a new song, this missionary team believes, is to offer a wider ecclesial embrace.

Our symposia agreed with that assessment. Being missionaries within secularity requires precisely that we build communities that are wide enough to include and hold our differences. What we are searching for is not a new technique, but a new sanctity; not a cooler dress and language, but a more inclusive embrace and vocabulary for the faith; not some updating of the gospel to make it more acceptable to today's world, but a more courageous radiating of its wide compassion; not some new secret that catches people's curiosity, but a way of following Christ that can hold more of the tensions of our world so that the world and our own children, irrespective of temperament and ideology, will find themselves more understood and embraced by what we hold deepest.[13]

Mission as Word and Spirit

What is our mission to and within secularity? What does it mean to be missionaries to our own children?

Michael Downey, in his keynote address, suggested that mission is not just another dimension of the church, one among others. In his view, it is not so much that the church has a mission, but more that the mission has the church.[14] Mission, the Second Vatican Council affirms, defines church.

Given the centrality and importance of mission, how might it be defined?

Jesus' mission, as seen in the Gospels, was that of announcing the reign or kingdom of God. But this kingdom, as St. Paul so graphically puts it, is "not a matter of eating and drinking, but of justice, peace, and the joy that is given by the Holy Spirit" (Rom. 14:17). In Jesus Christ, God came in word and spirit to try to bring this about, namely, to try to make truth and justice supreme in the world and peace and love supreme in our hearts. In essence, that was Jesus' mission.

And it is this mission that is entrusted to the church, and it is this same mission that is entrusted to us today as we seek to be missionaries within secularity. But how do we do that?

As Downey suggested in his keynote, we do not do this by trying to "sell Jesus" in the marketplace, by "dumbing down" the gospel, or by trying to make the Gospels more palatable to "spiritually hungry" people in a consumerist culture. Neither do we do it, Downey submits, by "facile appeals to authority." We do it rather by carrying on, by the testimony of our love and our lives, the mission of Jesus Christ, through word and spirit. How?

In word: The word of God, as incarnated in Jesus, needs to take on real flesh in our own bodies and lives and be the body of Christ on earth. Like Jesus, our lives must be our message and our lives must speak of and give real flesh to truth, justice, peace, love, holiness, and fidelity. When people look at our lives, what they see there must enable them to trust and to give themselves over in trust. The word needs to continue to have flesh in our lives. This is our real mission.

In spirit: The Holy Spirit, as we know, is the love and energy that flows between the Father and the Son. But this is not something abstract, but rather, as St. Paul tells us, is something that can be named. The Holy Spirit is charity, joy, peace, patience, kindness, generosity, fidelity, gentleness, and chastity (Gal. 5:22–23). To live in these is to live in the Holy Spirit. Conversely, St. Paul tells us, we should never delude ourselves that we are living in the Holy Spirit when our lives manifest immorality, hatred, rivalry, jealousy, anger, acts of selfishness, factionalism, and impurity (Gal. 5:19–21). When these are inside of us we are living in some other spirit, not God's spirit. We are missionaries to secularity, missionaries to our own children, when our lives radiate the love, joy, kindness, fidelity, and chastity that flow between the Father and the Son inside the life of the Trinity. To the degree that we manifest this, we will be effective missionaries.

We give the last word to Downey on this:

> Word is love heard and seen. Spirit is the principle of love's creativity and bonding. In the Son and the Holy Spirit, God is speaking and breathing. Word is what is said; Spirit is the saying. What is said in the saying is Love itself. But love expressed and bonding takes many different forms. To participate in the mission of Word and Spirit is to see and to share in the manifold manifestations of human expressivity and creativity as they disclose the divine reality. The Christian call is to flow with and in the missions of Word as expressivity and Spirit as creativity, communicating and bringing forth the one Love. In human expressivity and in various configurations of human creativity and bonding we come to know something of the magnitude of the God who is love. Our gift and task in mission is to cultivate, nurture, and sustain the great variety of the manifestations of the magnitude of God's love in all forms of expressivity and creativity. For human life and destiny are realized not in the exercise of individual rights and liberties, but in all those creative expressions of love that lead to a fuller communion in the one Love itself.[15]

Being a Prophetic Voice within Secularity

Secular culture, as we saw, is highly ambivalent. At one and the same time it is full of both grace and sin, angels and demons, moral insight and moral blind spots. Hence, to live and minister within secularity requires of us a strong prophetic element. We must bless the culture, but we must also challenge its blind spots, its moral inadequacies, and even its humanistic weaknesses. What are these?

Our weaknesses are often the underside of our strengths, and this is true for secular culture. Secular culture emphasizes human freedom, individual dignity, the innate value of the physical, private rights, material affluence as an ideal, access to comfort and entertainment, high tolerance, and high mobility. These are mostly good in themselves, but it is easy to lose the values and virtues needed to balance these off.

Hence, for the most part, secular culture struggles with excess, namely, an excess of reductionism, empiricism, mindlessness, individuality, grandiosity, narcissism, distraction, desire for comfort, cult around the human body, infidelity, and violence done in the name of God and truth. Everywhere we see decisions made, consciously and unconsciously, by a vision that focuses on this life only. With this comes a dumbing down of things, an itch for individuality that makes community impossible, an adolescent grandiosity that feels that God is not needed, a blindness to the Judeo-Christian roots undergirding our culture, a fixation on youth, physical health, and sexual attractiveness (as if they were salvation), a commitment to change, growth, and mobility that is the cause of untold betrayals in our commitments, a lack of concern about the poor and about mother earth that pours itself out instead as a moral fervor about lifestyle, and a propensity for distraction as a substitute for depth and interiority. Everywhere too we see violence being done in the name of God, morality, and truth.

What should be the specific elements of our prophecy inside of all of this?

Obviously, our prophecy, spoken with our lives and with our words, must speak out for the transcendent, for God, for a vision beyond just the here and now, for a vision of God's peace and nonviolence on this earth. We must, as was Martin Luther's dream, "make a protest for God." In doing this, we must speak for the soul, for depth, for interiority, for community, for a humility that recognizes real limits, for the poor, for mother earth, for fidelity, for a perspective that values salvation as being more than the enjoyment of youth, physical health, sexual pleasure, comfort, distraction, and lifestyle.

Our symposia named all these areas as places where prophetic challenge is needed, but it singled out four areas that it felt needed special emphasis:

* *Witness to the nonviolence of God*

In an age of increasing violence, fundamentalism, and the myth that God wishes to cleanse the planet of its sin and immorality by force, perhaps the first witness we must give to our world is a witness to God's nonviolence, a witness to the God revealed by Jesus Christ who opposes violence of all kinds, from war, to revenge, to capital punishment, to abortion, to euthanasia, to the attempt to use force to bring about justice and God's will in any way.

The first element of our prophecy, which must undergird everything else, is the nonviolence of a God who perennially challenges us with the words: "Let the one who is without sin cast the first stone" and who tells us that it is better to die unjustly and trust in God's redemption than to use force to bring about God's justice.

* *Forgiveness*

In a world and a culture that is full of wounds, anger, injustice, inequality, historical privilege, jealousy, resentment, bitterness, murder, and war, we must speak always and everywhere for forgiveness, reconciliation, and God's healing. Forgiveness lies at the center of Jesus' moral message. The litmus test for being a Christian is not whether one can say the creed and mean it, but whether one can forgive and love an enemy.

That concept is all but lost in our culture — and sometimes even in our churches. Thus, the second word in our prophecy, after we have spoken the word "God," should be the word "forgiveness."

◆ *Simplicity of life*

One of the major moral weaknesses inside of secularity is its consumerism, its greed for accumulation, affluence, comfort, and ever better lifestyle, coupled with an ever increasing dissatisfaction with what we own, have, and have achieved. There is an excess of consumption within secular cultures, and that excess is increasing rather than decreasing. As one of our key prophetic elements we must challenge our culture to simplicity of life. We must, by our own lifestyle and our words, help our culture to say these words: "I have enough! I am enough, as I am, with the life that has been given me. It is enough! It is enough to be able to breathe, as I am, to say a few words with my life."[16]

In a world where value is often judged by what one has accumulated and where there is too often a cancerous dissatisfaction with what one has achieved and acquired, Christian prophecy must point the way to simplicity of life.

◆ *The possibility of community beyond individuality and despite differences*

Secular culture struggles everywhere with community. Inside of secularity it is a struggle to make marriages work, families work, churches work, neighborhoods work, civic groups work, and even countries work. There is a constant pressure against community.

This pressure is rooted especially in two places: the excessive individuality inherent in modernity, and an ever increasing incapacity to live with each other in our differences.

We see signs of excessive individuality in secularity's increasing overfixation on privacy and individual rights. More and more, in one fashion or other, we hear the words: "This is my life, my love, my marriage, my home, my time, my business — and I will buy into family, community, church, and civic duty on my own terms."[17] We see this, for instance, in the refusal of so many young people today to get married. In their choice to simply live together, as opposed to making their relationship a public and sacramental reality, we hear an echo of René Descartes' lonely voice all those years ago, saying, "I think, therefore I am! . . . My reality is what's real, everything else is real only in relationship to my own reality."

How different this is from the concept of the body of Christ in scripture, where we are understood to be organically linked, interdependent parts of the same body, unable to live without each other. Our prophecy within secularity must speak out for the place of community, the body of Christ, marriage, family, church, parish, and even friendship.

Beyond our excessive individuality we are separated too by our differences and our wounds. We long for soulmates but find ourselves forever separated from each other by ideology, religion, race, gender, sexual orientation, wounds, bitterness, and historical accident. More and more, the tendency is to respond to this through a self-imposed apartheid, namely, we just stay away from each other in our differences and seek like-minded others with whom we can form community by huddling together in fear and loneliness.

What our prophecy needs to do is to model how community can be formed and sustained despite and beyond our differences and wounds. Our prophecy must challenge people to form community on the basis of what they are for rather than on the basis of what they are against. Fear of others, paranoia, and huddling together against what is different are increasing within secular culture. One of the most important things that Christianity has to say to secular culture is that real community is possible and that real community is living, working, and worshiping with those who are different from us.

Moreover, as we try to speak prophetic words within secularity we must be careful always that our prophecy issues

forth from the right source. True prophecy is always characterized by these marks: it will issue forth from love and not
from alienation;[18] it will not arise out of private grandiosity or
private agenda, but will ultimately come out of a community;
it will speak the crucified wisdom of the poor and see things
through their lens; and it will speak more about what it is for
than about what it is against.

The symposia also challenged its participants to not be
afraid, at times, to be countercultural in speaking out against
secularity's growing tendency (in politics, economics, and
social and religious theory) to understand itself as an "empire," and as a divinely willed "empire." God cannot be the
moral justification for imperialism or cultural or religious superiority of any kind. We applied this principle equally to
the church and the churches. Prophecy must also speak out
against any church or theology that understands itself as a
counter-empire.

Finally, and not insignificantly, the symposia felt that our
prophecy within secularity must, in its daily life, assume the
humble cloak of simple old-fashioned virtue: perseverance,
discipline, prayer, self-sacrifice, duty, chastity, and charity
which, in the end, reveal God's real face in our world.

Re-Imagining Our Ecclesial Structures

There is a curious anomaly inside our churches today within
most secularized cultures. On the one hand, we see finely
honed pastoral programs, an ever increasing theological liter-
acy, and parish structures that are ever more participatory and
inviting. Yet, on the other hand, we are witnessing constant
decline in church attendance. Our churches are emptying
and graying, even as we get better and better at what we are
offering through them. What is behind this?

Simply put, we are better at maintenance than at mission, better at knowing what to do with someone who walks
through a church door than we are at finding ways to get

people to walk through church doors. We do not lack good pastoral agents; we lack good missionaries. Our ecclesial structures, it would seem, are lacking the missionary element.

Our symposia posed the question: What is needed in terms of ecclesial structures? How can ecclesial structures better support the missionary dimension of Christianity?

One observation was that we must find new structures that again link the church vitally to the street. Part of the very definition of secularity is that institutions (schools, hospitals, orphanages, welfare centers, and the like) that formerly were operated by the churches have slowly been taken over by government agencies. In this shift, the church has lost a very important institutional presence in the lives of many people. We still have many faith-filled and dedicated Christians working in these areas, but we have less and less institutional presence in these areas of people's lives.

We recognized that this issue, while critically important, has no easy answer. It is one part of a bigger piece, the mammoth challenge to re-imagine our institutionalized presence within secularized culture. We see this, in miniature, in the case of certain religious orders that were founded to provide hospitals for the poor and find that today all their hospitals have been taken over by government and other secular agencies. How do they now re-imagine their charism and refound themselves on the basis of their original charism, namely, providing health care to the poor?

A new imagination is needed to refound ourselves institutionally on the streets on the basis of the gospel. This is a major challenge.

The symposia reflected too on the role of parishes. Parishes are the one huge ecclesial institution that has survived. But we asked ourselves: "Are we asking parishes to do too much? Are we overloading one structure with an impossible job description when we should be developing other ecclesial structures to handle some of these needs, particularly missiological needs?"

Gilles Routhier, whose keynote address is included in this book, suggested that we are indeed asking too much of our parish structures. He suggested that perhaps we should define some real limits, ask parishes to do the sacraments and to do them well, and then develop other ecclesial structures to do many of the things we are presently asking parishes to do.[19]

We looked too at the place and value of recent ecclesial and spiritual movements (Marriage Encounter, Cursillo, charismatic renewal, social justice groups, neo-catechumenate, Focalore, among others). We recognized their importance and their influence and suggested there is a lesson that can be extrapolated from their efforts, namely, that all of them, no matter their theology or approach, have three things in common: they foster and feed off an intensified sense of community, they try to give a certain clear form to life, and they call for a concrete set of actions. We noted that this was true too for many of the popular evangelical movements within Protestantism. We suggest that there are some important lessons to be learned from this in view of re-imagining our ecclesial structures.

One of our keynote speakers, Robert Barron, suggested that there are two other critical pieces that must be integrated into our imagination: the place of aesthetics and the place of popular religiosity.[20]

Barron pointed out that the sacramental imagination in Catholicism has always been predicated, among other things, on both an appeal to the physical senses (through beauty) and an appeal to the popular imagination through public religiosity (Corpus Christi–type processions and the like). What has happened to us, he suggested, is that we have become too timid in both areas. We have opted for functional rather than beautiful churches and we have, with few exceptions, all but negated huge public expressions of our faith. He pointed to the success of recent World Youth Days, which nobody predicted would draw such enthusiastic responses and influence popular culture as they did, as an example of a direction in which some of our answers might lie.

Another of our keynote speakers, Michael Downey, suggested that we might learn an important lesson from the L'Arche community as we try to re-imagine new ecclesial structures. Started some forty years ago by Jean Vanier, L'Arche establishes homes where people with developmental disability live in community with able-bodied people for mutual support and friendship. As the handicapped are welcomed into the community of the supposed healthy, they become the real teachers and the real nurturers of health. Moreover, they produce a situation that resists all labeling of right or left because, in L'Arche, the focus is unflinchingly on the human person and upon his or her dignity under God. In this, Downey submits, there is a critical lesson to be learned in terms of how the churches might approach secular culture.

In essence, as Walter Brueggemann put it, the task is to out-imagine the prevailing ways of understanding the relationship between secularity and Christianity. This task, we feel, calls for a new romantic imagination, that is, an imagination, like that of Francis and Clare of Assisi, that can romantically inflame the heart with the beauty of God and the faith. Our real task is to make the secular world fall in love with God again. We recognized that this will not be easy. Our churches are aging and graying, and many inside our churches and outside of them are already disillusioned with romance, love, and faith.

But, as Jesus tells us, nothing is impossible for God. Abraham and Sarah had a baby when he was a hundred years old and she was ninety. That child became their real heir and became the father of the faith for Muslims, Jews, and Christians alike. The real task, our symposia affirmed, is to get pregnant again by the Holy Spirit and in that gray-haired ecclesial pregnancy give birth to a new child that will be our true heir.

Notes

1. See notes 8 and 9 in chapter 1.

2. Jesus' final instruction in Matthew's Gospel: Matthew 28:19.

3. Gilles Routhier, in his keynote address in Ottawa, suggested that there are four aspects of the church that the secular mind still accepts: (1) the church as an agency to serve the poor, (2) the church as an agency to deliver the key rites of passage, (3) the church as an important voice within ethical discourse, and (4) the church as a "beautiful heritage." See Routhier's essay, chapter 8 in this book.

4. James Forbes, pastor of Riverside Church, New York City, quoted by Jim Wallis, *God's Politics: Why the Right Gets It Wrong and the Left Doesn't Get It* (San Francisco: HarperSanFrancisco, 2005), 16.

5. We noted, for example, how often in the case of mass murders within secular culture (e.g., the Oklahoma bombing, the Columbine massacre, the shootings at a McDonald's in San Diego) the murderers were ultimately acting out of a certain frustration at their own powerlessness.

6. Friedrich Nietzsche, *The Gay Science*, trans. W. Kaufmann (New York: Vintage Books, 1974).

7. Stephen Morris, *Catholic Register*, October 2, 2005, 31.

8. The paper this is quoted from, like the individual interventions made at that Synod, is not available. This particular quote is taken from an intervention by Bishop Michael Bzdel, Ukrainian rite bishop of Winnipeg, on the topic of immigrant Catholicism (as recorded in the private notes of Ronald Rolheiser, who was with the Canadian bishops as a peritus at that 1997 Synod).

9. Several symposia participants pointed to the theology and spirituality of Pierre Teilhard de Chardin as a possible model vis-à-vis holding this tension in a more wholesome way, particularly to the principles he enunciates in *Le milieu divin*, where he speaks of having two "incurable loves," one for the world and one for God, and how a deep sense of the oneness of all things prevents him from ever sacrificing one for the other.

10. This was the substance of Ronald Rolheiser's theme-setting address in San Antonio in 2004. His presentation was entitled "The Scope of Our Ecclesial Embrace: What Kind of Ecclesiology Best Undergirds Our Mission to Secularity?" See *Seattle University Review* (Fall 2005).

 11. Some key fragments of our conversations on this are worth noting here:

- The "middle" can be just as much an ideological location as either the right or the left.
- Both "liberals" and "conservatives" protect valuable truths, just as both have their particular blind spots. In oversimplified terms, here are some of the strengths and weaknesses of each:

  1. Strengths of liberalism:

     - its feel for the world's life-pulse, its color, and its strengths
     - its valuing of freedom, democracy, equality, individual rights
     - its agenda, when it's at its best, for social justice
     - its tolerance

  2. Strengths of conservativism:

     - its sense of the sacred, the holy, the other world
     - its call for self-sacrifice
     - its sense that we do need some "taboos"
     - its sense of archetypal structure and anthropological tradition

- But our greatest strengths are also, often times, our greatest weaknesses. We recognized too these particular tendencies within liberal and conservative ideology:

  1. Weaknesses of liberalism:

     - its naiveté about the power of energy, particularly sexual energy
     - its occasional carelessness about private morality
     - its present fall from its own agenda, i.e., the move from promoting justice for the poor to its advocacy of lifestyle
     - its adolescent grandiosity toward its own moral origins
     - its too easy loss of the sense of duty and self-sacrifice

  2. Weaknesses of conservativism:

     - its habitual fear of too many things, not least of sexuality
     - its fear of freedom

- its tendency to sell out freedom for authority and order
- its habitual color, as timid and legalistic
- its moral blind spot in the area of social justice

It is time for both the right and left to admit that they have run out of imagination, that the categories of conservative and liberal are not useful, and that what is needed is a radicalism that takes us beyond both the right and the left. That radicalism can be found only in the gospel that is neither liberal or conservative but fully compassionate.

12. This mission is alive and well today. Two other missionaries are living and working with the original four, making for a community of six. They publish a small newsletter detailing part of their ongoing growth. The newsletter can be obtained upon request. Email: *jstaakomi@aol.com*.

13. To achieve this more fully will mean recognizing that there are certain innate tensions within all ecclesial communities and that these must be respected so that one pole of the tension may not be sacrificed to the other for purposes of clarity, legalism, less tension, ideology, liturgical or doctrinal purity, or because of the temperament of a given community, pastor, bishop, or zeitgeist. These tensions stem from the innate structure of ecclesial community itself and, for that reason, will always be with us. They are like gauges on a complex instrument panel. Our task is to monitor the gauges and set them properly.

What are these innate tensions?

* The liberal in tension with the conservative

* The theological in tension with the devotional

* The liturgical in tension with the pastoral

* The Eucharist in tension with the Word

* Private morality in tension with social justice

* The prophetic in tension with institutional structures

* Compassion in tension with the programmatic

* Missionary in tension with maintenance

* Denominational commitment in tension with ecumenism

* Christian commitment in tension with other religions

* Individual charism in tension with community needs

* Aesthetics in tension with simplicity of life

- Letting ourselves be evangelized by the world in tension with being Christian missionaries carrying the message and person of Jesus Christ

- Being "set apart from" in tension with "being in identity with" the larger community

- The quest for personal holiness in tension with the wider ecclesial agenda of the community we belong to

14. See Michael Downey's essay, chapter 6 in this book.

15. Ibid. See below p. 122.

16. Mary Jo Leddy, *Radical Gratitude* (Maryknoll, NY: Orbis Books, 2002). Not a direct quote, but a paraphrase.

17. Reginald Bibby points out that we can see a remarkable similarity between how adult children today treat their own families and how they treat their own churches, namely, they want them to exist and to be there for them at special times (e.g., rites of passage and special celebrations), but they don't want them around on a day-to-day basis. They want to pick and choose when they want them, and they want to buy in on their own terms.

18. Daniel Berrigan's book on prophecy, *Ten Commandments for the Long Haul* (Nashville: Abingdon, 1981), puts this well. "A prophet," Berrigan says, "makes a vow of love, not of alienation."

19. See Gilles Routhier's essay, chapter 8 of this book. In another presentation, Routhier pointed out how we are focusing more and more on parishes alone by highlighting how, in the 1960s, in Quebec (and in North America in general) about one-third of all priests were in non-parish ministry. Today that is no longer the case, and more and more the ordained priesthood is being identified with parish ministry only and, within the parish structure, that ministry is being defined ever more as belonging inside the sanctuary.

20. See Robert Barron's presentation, chapter 9 of this book.

Chapter Four

FRAGMENTS OF
OUR CONVERSATIONS

MICHAEL MEADE, a mythologist and professional story-teller, often tells his audiences that one of the ways to enter a story is to focus in on the one detail that, for whatever reason, most caught your attention. That particular detail may not in fact be a significant part of the story and other aspects of the story may become more important to you later on, but at that moment, that detail which has created a little shock wave inside you is where the story and your life intersect. It is important that such a little detail be picked up and examined.

We would like to simply list a series of sound bites, fragments from our conversations, that for whatever reason caught the attention of our participants and caused some little shock waves. Some carried more substance than others, some were more serious than others, and some caused more stir than others, but each one made itself felt.

With this in mind, here are some fragments from our conversations:

- In an insecure time, clarity counts for more than truth!
- God isn't in trouble just because the churches are!
- Partially, we must unlearn our training to make more direct contact with a resistant secularity.
- Spirituality is people's birthright.

- People go where they get fed.

- Recovering the tradition is a great labor.

- We must seek to recover the core, heart, of our tradition, beyond its encrusted accretions, and then put our own passion to that heart.

- Scripture and tradition have been around life's questions for a long time and know their excesses and know what you can do and what you can't.

- To enter the conversation with secularity we must first retrieve the depths of our own tradition; we must take hold of our own identity again, before we can become relevant. More specifically, we must recover the feminine, be more gentle around holy eros within people's lives, re-present the sacraments, recover the mystical, respect the depth of intellect, and heal the split between faith and the culture. To quote Rumi: "We must gamble everything for love."

- We must work at finding our own faith-voice and then learn to speak in an invitational way.

- We must work at developing a profound ascesis of listening.

- You can only give away what you have become and transform others to the depth that you yourself have experienced transformation.

- We are in exile, but we should remember that all transformation happens in exile because that is the only time God can get at us. We need exile to free us from power, possessiveness, prestige, and the performance principle.

- All great spiritualities are about letting go.

- We have been churched, but we haven't read the gospel.

- A weeping mode is different from a fixing mode.

- Gaze upon the one whom you have pierced and gaze long enough until you get it!

- Stay with the pain, the exile, the kenosis, until it changes you. Hold the mystery long enough for it to change you.

- We come to God more by doing it wrong than by doing it right.

- We are both the crucified Christ and the resurrected Christ, and thus we can be joyful and sing, even now!

- We are at a new place in the West regarding Christianity. We must create something new. "Adaptation" may not be enough. We must risk doing a new thing.

- We must be careful that our visioning is not just about the deployment of personnel and clergy.

- Perhaps we are asking the parish to carry too many things, asking it to do something it can no longer do. Parish and mission are not coterminous.

- There are four aspects of the church that people still do accept: (1) The church as an agency to serve the poor; (2) the church to deliver the rites of passage; (3) the church as a certain voice within ethical discourse; and (4) the church as a beautiful heritage — but we must be careful to not let ourselves be identified with only these.

- We must make the gospel known "through small veins." But we need too to make the gospel known "through the big veins" of social institutions, through institutional presence in health, education, politics, the arts, and economics.

- We need committed Christians in the marketplace, not just in the sacristy and sanctuary.

- We must commit ourselves and our efforts not just to the baptized, but also to all people of sincerity and good will.

- We must dream of new ecclesial "houses," namely, neighborhood houses, houses of culture, houses of charity, and houses of prayer.

- We need to move from the logic of adaptation to the logic of creation.

- Mission is participation in God's breathing out of word and spirit.

- To share in the mission of Christ, of word and spirit, does not always mean using words about Jesus.

- The fact that some ground is hostile or indifferent does not absolve us from the mandate to keep on sowing, though perhaps we need to do so with more patience, listening, love, and solicitude.

- Certain aspects of secularity — affluence, materialism, individuality, tolerance, and democratic process — are, *in se*, good, but we must also beware of their underside.

- Two elements of secularity are antithetical to the gospel, namely, low esteem for life and materialistic consumerism.

- We can live without faith and we can even live without love, but we can't live without hope.

- God is "ad/vent/ing." . . . God came, comes, and is coming!

- Depression tells you that the way you have been doing things up to now is not okay.

- The secular world, too much, finds our theological language and symbol as "scmantically empty."

- The gospel is ultimately about the poor. We may never lose this non-negotiable imperative.

- Since where we live largely determines what we see, we must listen to the poor. They give us a crucified wisdom because they are at the foot of the cross, watching a slow dying.

- When money goes up, human rights go down!

- Part of evangelization is the movement to eliminate poverty.

- Nothing is worse than someone else wanting good in your place!

- Religious communities are big international bodies and could do a lot, internationally, as regards poverty.

- In our secular society often the social movements cannot do enough effectively when they have an explicit Christian or faith label. Hence, the implied need to base ourselves more on a solidarity grounded within humanity itself.

- There are human foundations, solid ones, for moral progress within our culture, and we need to accept this and widen the pool of sincere people with whom we form one body to work for a better world. Excessive denominational identification can narrow the body.

- Exclude exclusiveness!

- Faith is not certitude. We don't need to know because God knows.

- Secularity is both a restriction of consciousness and a widening and freeing of it; what there is of it is good, but there is a lot missing! Secularity is interested spiritually, but is largely spiritually illiterate.

- A huge question within secularity is: How does one become spiritual without leaving behind the realm of the physical, the psychological/emotional, the sexual, the incarnate?

- Jesus offers us a model; he tries to move us from one state to another: we are asleep, and he tries to wake us; we are deaf, and he tries to open our ears; we are dumb, and he tries to open our mouths to speech and praise; we are narrow, and he tries to widen our perspective; we are blind, and he tries to open our eyes; we are lost, and he tries to find us; and we are dead, and he tries to resurrect us. This must be our model within a secularized world.

- How do you get awake? By doing concrete spiritual action in the concrete material world. The spiritual needs to penetrate the physical and the social.

- Our dullness withholds gifts unimagined.

- We wake up through prayer: prayer is resistance to temptation. You must actively reach out into the other world or this world will drown you. God's will is always the offer of endless possibilities, but you have to stay awake and pray. Jesus says: "Rise, pray!"

- If you stay awake and pray, "an angel" will strengthen you, that is, you will be strengthened from the other world.

- It is hard to grasp the spiritual realm because of our pre-occupations and anxieties. Among these, to be highlighted, are our addictions to power and comfort. These can be a culpable blindness — and are a terrible restriction of consciousness.

- We can be asleep out of depression, "sheer sorrow."

- When the sun shines right, even the meanest trees sparkle.

- The cock will crow at the breaking of your own ego; there are lots of ways to wake up!

- The seed falls in the soil and we are, each one of us, all four kinds of soil: (1) We are the soil by the side of the road — where the birds eat the seed before it has a chance to root. This refers to our failure of attention. (2) We are rocky ground — we receive the word with great joy but don't have the depth to sustain it, especially in time of persecution and trial. We lose the word through our failure to be able to handle contradiction. (3) We are the soil where the seed grows together with the thorns which eventually choke out the seed. The seed has to transform the thorns and not simply grow alongside them. (4) We are too the good soil.

- A special energy can be found where things seem to be in contradiction. When we search for where the wells of energy might be concealed, we should search at places where we experience tension.

- As human beings we habitually experience various dual-ities: light and darkness, finite and infinite, words and silence, masculine and feminine, human and divine. When we hold these in proper tension we experience healthy energy; when we do not hold them in proper tension we create unhealthy dualisms. The incarnation is the place where we see precisely how these dualities are held in proper tensions.

+ Jesus is the imaginative poet who patterns for us how we should hold everything that is inside of our experience in proper tension.

+ What we see in Jesus is a stunning imagination, an imagination that loves what is incomplete and loves places of energy. It is because we incarnate this so badly as church that so many artists leave the church. In essence, we have domesticated Jesus' imagination, and present inertia in the church is very much a failure of imagination.

+ The key to the divine imagination is the Trinity. We can never understand the Trinity, but we can experience it.

+ We need to pray, minister, and live out our spirituality with more imagination, namely, with more originality, more evoking of God's presence beneath the surface of things, more risk, more commitment to the justice of wholeness, more daring to embrace what's human, more traveling to sin and guilt and lingering there, and more loyalty to the mystery of form.

+ We must use a renewed imagination to tap into the depth of spiritual hunger that lies at the heart of secularity and make sure that we do not reduce spirituality to morality. There has been a tragic "non-conversation" between the spiritual hunger in the culture and the custodians of a great spiritual tradition.

+ To move beyond churches that are weary, gray, and tired, we must also move beyond clericalism, fear of the feminine, an excessive dis-ease with eros, reification of authority, and reclaim both our mystical and our intellectual traditions.

◆ We must put ourselves back in sync with what's best in our tradition of the sacraments.

◆ Evangelization begins with the recognition that the gospel is "good news" and that a culture or church that ignores that fact is dull and asleep and needs to be awakened.

◆ There are three elements to evangelization: (1) a turning toward God; (2) a turning that affects both individuals, and the society and culture; and (3) a turning that is ultimately caused by the power of the gospel and the Holy Spirit. Evangelization has to happen at three levels: (1) the renewal of the evangelizers themselves; (2) a calling back of those who have heard the gospel, but among whom it has not taken hold or has been lost in some way; (3) a calling of those who have not yet heard the gospel.

◆ Inside of the church we are not homogeneous, that is, we are not one generation but are two and a half generations within one generation.

◆ We should carefully observe how various countercultural groups are engaging secularity: fundamentalists, enthusiasm movements, social justice groups, the new conservatives. All these groups, which come from both the right and the left, have three things in common: (1) they foster and feed off an intense sense of community; (2) they try to give clear form to life; (3) they call for particular sets of actions.

◆ We need a new apologetics, with these traits: an intelligible language, Christ as central, a "Catholic sacramental" view of the world, and a valuing of the importance of narrative because that is how people construct their identities.

◆ We must be careful not to see the new conservatism as simply a pathology. There are important reasons why so many people, especially young people, are drawn to it, and we must, with courage, examine those reasons and learn from them.

- We need to begin our proclamation with what lies at the center of our faith, namely, that Jesus Christ has died and has risen. Jesus is the icon of the invisible God, God's pattern of being in the world.

- We begin by announcing Jesus Christ as crucified as a way of telling the culture that not all is right with us, namely, the author of life came and we killed him. But concomitant with that announcement we also proclaim that Jesus has risen from the dead. Jesus wasn't just the one who was crucified by the world; he is also the one who rises from the dead, shows us his wounds, and announces peace.

- Our evangelization must be predicated on this insight: in the old order of things, we believe that violence and evil come into the world and they are to be gotten rid of by a morally superior violence. But in the new order of things, in Jesus, justice and peace are restored not through violence but through empathy and forgiveness. We kill God, but God returns in a forgiving love, and this is what opens up a new world.

- Everything that is good participates in the energy and color of God.

- America was shaped by Calvin and Hobbes!

- We may not continue to keep our faith private. Evangelization must show itself publicly — like the medieval pilgrimages and processions and today's World Youth days. Faith must be expressed publicly and in colorful, romantic ways. We must stop building "beige churches" and build churches that express public faith.

- We are better than we know and worse than we think.

- To many of today's generation the texts of scripture no longer speak and only the text of life itself speaks.

- We can learn something from the effectiveness of John Paul II's message to youth: "You matter! You can make a difference! You face a great moral challenge!"

- We are drowning in individuality, especially as it pertains to sustaining and passing on our faith. To sustain a faith life today involves more than a vague human connection; it must be supported in a real human connection — church, family, community.

- We must listen to our contemplatives: our poets, artists, mystics, and returning missionaries. They will help tell us what's best and worst in secularity and help us form an alternative imagination. There has always been an alternative imagination to the "myth of progress," and Catholics have much to offer in terms of giving such an alternative vision.

- Unless we can regain our own inner vision and define ourselves more by what we are for than by what we are against, we will continue to divide from each other and will always make war.

- Within secularity, the ideal of a good life has been too much replaced by the vision of having more. Liberal ideology has become too privatized and conservative ideology too re-entrenched in authority and rules.

- September 11 has helped define the present moment, and we must access that, especially as it points to our mortality.

- What Catholicism offers is a tradition, a long tradition that throws light on history and upon realities beyond the here and now and, most importantly, points to world community. Catholicism calls us to world citizenship, beyond our own backgrounds.

- We are "secularity," and so we should ask ourselves some questions: (1) Are we sufficiently aware, and critical enough, of the fact that secularity has largely shaped our own imaginations? (2) How much does secularity shape our own view and criticism of the church? (3) Do we have the same incapacity for conversation with what's other to us as does secularity? (4) Do we really listen sympathetically to "the

other," including other Catholics who are of a different ecclesial ideology? (5) Are we caught up in patterns of thinking
that are emotionally satisfying, but are blocking dialogue
with those who think differently than we do? (6) Do we ever
move toward those who are not "like-minded"?

+ Our task is to find a new way to imagine the whole so that
we keep all the polarities and tensions within it.

+ Fundamentalism, in its reaction to modernity and post-
modernity, does not create a large enough imaginative
construct to hold the whole.

+ Youth often focus on more traditional ecclesial things (like
Eucharistic adoration) since these can, in a way, give them
a "still point" in their world of flux.

+ Sometimes we find the good secularity in the world and the
bad secularity in the church.

+ Christianity isn't dying. What is dying are some assumptions about modernity and the church.

+ The church, too often, outside of its official doctrines,
gives us the same narrative as the world: success, power,
winning!

+ Mission has the church, not vice versa; that is, mission
is Jesus and the Holy Spirit and what they are doing in
human hearts. This must define the church.

+ Secularity is not a "pathology"; it has helped contribute
wonderfully to our moral understanding. For example: (1) it
has highlighted human dignity, human freedom, human
rights; (2) it has helped create both the freedom *from* religion and the freedom *for* religion; (3) it has highlighted
intellectual freedom; (4) it has helped highlight too the
voices of all peoples; (5) it has helped the world move
beyond the claim that truth lies in "authority alone."

+ A daydream: we are celebrating the fortieth anniversary
of *Gaudium et Spes* and the birth of L'Arche. L'Arche

welcomed the handicapped into the community of the supposed healthy. They, the handicapped, are "the other," but they are the real teachers; they teach us what it means to be human. And this resists labeling, of left or right. Why? Because it, unflinchingly, focuses on the human person and his or her dignity. What might we learn from this model vis-à-vis our dialogue with secularity?

+ We must be more attentive to young people's desire for sacraments, scripture, and catechesis.

+ Our task is not a new one; the early church had to maintain itself within an empire, and the Jewish communities prior to that had to maintain themselves and their religious practices within a pluralistic context.

+ We face two temptations: (1) conservative: play it too safe, create safe conclaves for ourselves; (2) liberal: lose ourselves within secularity.

+ The church has to "out-imagine" secularity, and scripture is that alternative imagination.

+ Technology is replacing imagination.

+ The church should affirm the human spirit and recover a sense of the "holy" that unmasks our easy absolutism. We have easy absolutes, even as everyone is questioning unendingly about everything.

+ Take the advice of Deuteronomy 6:7: "Wear your children out with instruction."

+ We need to tell "narratives of miracles" and "oracles of holiness" so that our eyes become used again to seeing the action of God in everyday life.

+ The church is the only place in town where an alternative vision can be uttered.

+ We live and minister among people who are devoured by anxiety. Prophetic faith is an antidote to anxiety. When is the last time someone said, "Do not fear!" with any credibility?

- So much of the atheism of our time is little more than "teenagers ranting at their parents!"

- We have "seasons of sub-Christian faith."

- Get a life, and live it with a neighbor!

- The church may not become just another place for frightened people to hide.

- The church is excessively preoccupied with matters that are not so important.

- Jeremiah 29 tells us to "pray for the peace of Babylon, because that is your place." For us that translates into, "Pray for the peace of the world, because that is our place."

- The antidote to torture (and the paranoia it bespeaks) is the Eucharist and the trust and community it can create.

- When you sign on with the God of life in a death-system, the death-system will try to kill you!

- In the secular world, we don't face torture, but we have reality TV, and that amounts to about the same thing.

PART THREE

Background Resources

Chapter Five

PATHWAYS TO NEW EVANGELIZATION IN THE FIRST WORLD

Robert Schreiter, C.PP.S.

W E NEED TO LOOK more closely at the situation in which we are presenting the gospel: how people might, or might not, hear it. This is a crucial area in missiology that has gained more and more attention. People can think they know what they are saying, but the situation may call for a very different reality. The bishops' Special Synod of 1973 was devoted to evangelization. Out of that, in 1974 came Pope Paul VI's Apostolic Exhortation *Evangelii Nuntiandi*, On Evangelization in the Modern World. That remains the signature text for evangelization within the Roman Catholic Church. He proposed that evangelization is more than getting the words right. It's what happens when those words come to the ears of hearers. In 1983, Pope John Paul II called for a "new evangelization." Evangelization understood the way the U.S. bishops proposed in a letter in 1992 involves three elements. It involves, first, a turning to God, a conversion. In other words, you're not the same after you have heard the Word of God. You find yourself coming to a new place. Second, it affects both individuals and society. It's not simply that individuals find themselves turning to Christ; it also has an effect on society itself. John Paul II has developed that particularly in his concepts of a "civilization of love" and "a culture of life" in the 1990s. The third element of evangelization is to remember that what caused this change in individuals and societies is the power of the gospel and of the Holy Spirit. That is to say, we are but agents. We are not the ones who effect the change. What we do is create the space or environment in which the gospel then is able to act.

John Paul II saw the new evangelization happening at three levels. First of all, it has to do with the renewal of the evangelizers themselves. Paul VI suggests this in paragraph 18, an often forgotten part of *Evangelii Nuntiandi.* The church has to be undergoing conversion itself if it hopes to be an effective messenger. Second, it's a calling back of those who have heard the gospel, but in whom the gospel has not taken sufficient root. The third group that we most frequently associate with new evangelization is those who have never heard the gospel at all. John Paul shared his own thoughts on this in 1991, in his encyclical *Redemptoris Missio.* The one element that caught a lot of people's imagination was paragraph 37, where he talks about the new *areopagoi,* going back to the story of Paul in the Areopagus in Acts 19, saying that we have to find out where people are converging in modern societies. That's the place where we need to bring the gospel, rather than just simply preaching in our churches and hoping somebody will come in. When we talk about evangelization in the first world, among those three audiences, there is a special emphasis on the second audience, on those people who may have heard something about the gospel, but in whose lives and in whose society this has not taken root. To be sure, there are those who have never heard the gospel in first-world societies and, of course, those of us who live in them need renewal. That's simply by way of background. I want to turn, then, principally to pathways.

We need a kind of reconnaissance of the terrain that we're talking about when we use the word "secularization." The term "secularization" first grew up in the idea of the alienation of church property by the state. Property went over from the church into the secular sphere. For most of us, it's tied up with the kind of emancipation of reason and the individual that took place during the Enlightenment and the consequent forms of modernity, of living in a modern world. It has meant, second, a separation of the church out of the discourse that is going on in the public forum, and consequently religion becomes a more privatized affair. In other words, it's left up to the individual to be engaged in religion. Part of the implication of that is that the individual is free not to participate in religious activity. At the beginning of the twentieth century, it resulted in a kind of secularization hypothesis that the world would become increasingly disenchanted with the idea that the world, beyond the visible realities, was also surrounded by an invisible transcendent reality. It would begin as simply an individual affair and would gradually reach a vanishing point by which time religion would disappear altogether. Many sociologists of religion took up this idea. An important element to be aware of is that this sense of autonomy grew out of Christian theology. So secularization is not an alien force from the outside, but something that grew up within Christianity itself.

The meaning of what secularity is today creates a very different terrain. First, I'm going to call this terrain an uneven terrain. Second, it's an uncertain terrain. It's unclear what its exact future is going to be. This became apparent starting around 1990. In 1993, a number of sociologists from the United States and Europe got together in a kind of quasi-secret meeting in Rotterdam. The theme of the meeting was "Secularization: How Did We Get It So Wrong?" I think there are three major points that have come out of how the scene has shifted in the last ten years. There is the realization that you cannot measure secularization simply by church attendance. This was a kind of major empirical index. We watched

the decline of church attendance. But there was a realization that there was still a lot of very strong, diffuse belief
in the supernatural throughout the whole range of the first
world. Grace Davies caught it in the title of a book she wrote
on British religions since 1945, which she called *Believing
without Belonging.* "Where are people actually on the issue
of belief?" They believe in the autonomy of the individual
and freedom of choice. They accept the often unspoken assumption that the task of each of us in a secular society is
to construct ourselves. That is to say, who our parents were,
what they did, the background we came out of is interesting
only to a point. It's what we do with ourselves that becomes
important. Part of that pattern was that you had to remake or
unmake any religious commitments you had, usually starting around age eighteen, which is not the ideal time to be
thinking about these kinds of things. So we are seeing patterns of people leaving the churches starting around that age.
This goes back to 1920; it's not something that happened exclusively in the 1970s and 1980s. So just measuring church
attendance was not an adequate way of doing it, particularly
in an individualistic society where people were constructing
themselves.

In 1990, there was a resurgence of religious sensibility,
carried by an upsurge of immigration caused by the globalization of the time. In Europe and the United States, the 1990s
had the largest immigration in American and European history. These immigrations were strongest in the first world.
The most multicultural society in the world is Australia. The
United States is the second, and Canada is the third. Immigrants bring their religion with them. The 1965 Immigration
Act allowed Asians into the United States for the first time
in considerable numbers. There was considerable prejudice
against having Asians in the United States prior to that time.
So immigration brought an upsurge of religion, and this is perhaps most evident in Europe, where former churches are being

turned into mosques or simply being used for other purposes: movie theaters, garages, warehouses, and nightclubs.

The second feature is the rise of Pentecostalism. Pentecostalism is the fastest-growing form of Christianity in the world today. Most Pentecostals today become Pentecostals through evangelization by other Pentecostals from their own country. These are not just the poor. Pentecostalism is also a middle-class phenomenon. I say this because people are finding their own ways to negotiate the relationship of modernity (read "secularity") and Christianity. It is not possible to simply write off Pentecostalism as we once did popular religiosity in Latin America. It is not a kind of deficit form of Christianity, that is to say, "If these people were better evangelized, smarter, or more mentally healthy they'd be just like us." That's not what's happening. I think we have to be very careful about writing off groups, even fundamentalist groups, by saying that they're a pathology. I think we have to be able to see what's going on behind this phenomenon.

The third element in the resurgence of religion was the very persistence of religion itself. To measure religion only by church attendance represents a particular perspective, a perspective largely of the clergy, whose occupation is to have people in churches on Sunday. It doesn't get in touch with what is sustaining people in their lives. All kinds of religiosity persist, and from a doctrinal point of view people can be massively illiterate, but the feeling is there. Secularization may represent what happens under particular social conditions that are not being reproduced in the same way in different parts of the world. So people are engaging modernity and secularity in very different ways in diverse parts of the world.

Europe is the heartland of secularity. Here secularity is seen in its strongest form, with the possible exception of Australia. One of the most perceptive Danish sociologists has written about the situation in Denmark, and by extension Sweden, less so Norway. There they have "belonging without believing." If you were born in Sweden, you were automatically a

member of the Church of Sweden. You didn't have to be baptized. All you needed was a birth certificate. That's changed
now. But the sense of the "folk church" was immensely strong.
You have people growing up who are taught religion in the
schools but have no religious affiliation. Much of it becomes
very marginal. If you hear them trying to engage in biblical
narratives, they get it all mixed up. You have the situation of
strongly Catholic countries like Spain and Italy, where secularization has happened very rapidly. There's even hostility
toward organized religion in these countries because people
are still trying to distinguish themselves in different ways.

Poland is grappling with rapid secularization. Enrollment
in seminaries over the last ten years has dropped about 50 percent. In other countries, the forty years of communism have
resulted in two generations who have no faith at all. Sixty
percent of all burials in Germany today are done without any
ritual whatsoever. People are simply disposed of in cemeteries. There are no monuments, there are no markers; there
are trees. The cemeteries look like golf courses. People know
their loved ones are in there somewhere, but they cannot
visit the gravesite. There's been a keen interest among young
people in religion where it was repressed most brutally, particularly in the Czech Republic. It's coming up in a different
way. Australia has never been a particularly religious country. Those parts of Australia that started as penal colonies
have no stake in supporting the established church. The secularity there is perhaps the strongest, but it's not a hostile
secularity. The United States and Canada present a somewhat different case. One of the perplexing things for most
Europeans is how religious it is in the United States, even
though there has never been an established church. I think
one of the things that make it difficult to evangelize in Europe is the memory of an established church and the fact that
in some countries the churches with attendance of less than
10 percent are massively subsidized by the state. The largest
employer in Germany is the church. Because of the church the

Germans have loads of funds, and they're very generous with others. I'm not faulting Germany, but as people are taking themselves off the rolls in terms of religious affiliation, this is having a precipitous effect on how the churches are doing.

A second feature is the Enlightenment. Europe was largely influenced by the French Enlightenment, where there was a tremendous struggle with the church. Much of the Enlightenment in the United States was formed by the Scottish Enlightenment. Princeton University was staffed with Edinburgh graduates when it began. That's a much more relaxed understanding of reason, which is not necessarily hostile to religion. Moreover, many people who came to the United States at certain stages were victims of religious persecution. So holding on to faith was a much more important element of who they were.

Everything in the United States gets turned into a market. You have the marketplace of competing denominations; there are over nine hundred forms of Protestantism. You have competition in a way that is not the case in Europe. Canada is in some ways an in-between place. Quebec, which was solidly Catholic until about thirty years ago, has seen a kind of secularization not unlike that of Europe. Reginald Bibby, one of the major followers of Canadian religiosity, discovered a lot more religiosity than he thought was there. What can be said about these contexts? Migration is having an important effect. It was announced yesterday that a major concern, especially for the Missionary Oblates here, is the concern about evangelization of the poor. Many of the poor in our countries, apart from first-nation peoples, are migrants. Immigrant religion shows that religion is an important bridge between where people came from and where they are now, at least for the first generation. The second generation is more problematic. Globalization, while providing some overarching understandings of the human being and society, is being found by many people to be grossly inadequate. It's based upon largely consumerist models. Your value as a human being is determined by what you can make or produce and what you can consume, in the reverse order, actually. What you can consume and what you can produce. To the extent you can't do that, you're not worth nearly as much.

A third, more slippery generalization one can make about the first world is this thing called post-modern. "Postmodern" is defined in different ways, and its prevalence is not uniform throughout the first world. What the post-modern does in one form or another is to react to the shortcomings of the modern. The idea of progress in the 1960s, when we believed that we were really going to be able to change the world, is much chastened by the present — the disjuncture of different parts of life caused by pluralism, the way people are thrown together, the way people are confronted, particularly wealthy people, with a variety of choices with no clear criteria about which choice might be optimal for them. People end up not making choices at all or making them only halfheartedly, so they make a change simply to move on to something else. The end reflects the loss of the big narratives, the big stories that hold our lives together. The fragmenting of the big narrative causes people to create a sort of arbitrary collage out of various elements to explain their lives. "Multiple identities" and "hybrid identities" are terms being used. It has to do with how long people have been involved with secularity, the pace at which it is happening, and the history in which it is found between generations.

In the first generation, and many of us here in this room would be counted among that, we find a much more adversarial relationship with the church. I think it's important to think about what extent we're using that lens to talk about secularity because demographers tell us that we are reactionaries of the right or the left. You can be on either end by saying, "These young people are so conservative, they don't understand anything," or by saying, "The world is going to hell in a handbasket." I think a lot of the first generation is that way.

The second generation, many of them, has grown up without any sense of religion at all. If you live in a prosperous society, you can probably get by that way. You have to deal with individual tragedy, but nothing terribly large. The third generation that's coming of age today, in many instances, is curious about religion and is open to it as a possibility. Part of it is the post-modern thing. Religion becomes one option alongside many others. There's not a world of just two things, the right way and the wrong way. There are all kinds of possibilities. Even in the more difficult places like secular Europe we see this. There is an openness we're seeing that was not the case before. The children of immigrants present a special case. If the previous generation was absent or hostile, there's a greater likelihood that the present generation is going to be interested. Thus, when we talk about secularity today, we have to talk about age and generation as well as context. This is a paradox in a "post-survival society" concerning people who are relatively comfortable. On the one hand, they engage in a search for meaning, often on their own terms. On the other hand, they are suspicious of institutions. That's where we find preaching the gospel today, somewhere between those particular points.

Let me close this second and longest part by giving you three images of the secular. The first is the one that's most common, that religion is receding. It's like a piece of landmass that's being eroded, getting smaller and smaller all the time. It's the privatization, the disappearance of religion. A second image that has emerged in the 1990s is that secularity is a kind of thin veneer, that if you poke through it, there's a teeming religiosity underneath it that may not be to your liking or the way you would configure it, but it's there. The third image that's emerging now and needs more exploration is that of secularity as an island within religiosity. They are flowing into each other in different kinds of ways. Political scientists are scrambling at the moment to come up with ways of understanding world order and disorder with religion as a factor because all the former models were largely secular; they all came out of the first world and the attempt to find where religion fits into that. These models reveal receding religion with secularity as a level, layer, or veneer, but with realities below and secularity within religiosity.

I'd like to identify for you just a couple of pathways without going into much detail. In the new edition of his book *Models of Contextual Theology*, Steve Bevans speaks of the "countercultural model." This can be traced back to Leslie Newbigin, a Reformed minister who went as a missionary to India in 1936 and was one of the founders of the Church of South India. He returned to Britain in 1974 and was appalled by what he saw. He said, "I spent many years as a missionary to India to bring Christianity, and I find now that it's largely disappeared in Britain." He began a number of initiatives that led to a movement in England called the "Gospel of Culture Project" and its larger counterpart here in North America, the United States and Canada, called the "Gospel and Our Culture Network." On the continent in Europe, there's also "Missiology and Western Culture." These groups work largely out of a Reformed Christian or Calvinist view of the world, which emphasizes the sovereignty of God over creation. Creation here is seen in its corruptness and its need for salvation. The result is a highly critical view of the state of Western culture and a call back to the gospel. In the English-speaking part of the world, because you can do this in English, there is a kind of polemic against Christendom. This is because we have two words, "Christendom" and "Christianity," or their equivalents, in many languages. In European languages, there's only one word for both. It takes a kind of dark Johannine view of the world, the way it's talked about in John's Gospel. There is some Catholic participation in this, particularly in Europe; however, I think the view is distinctively Reformed in that regard.

Some of the strategic pathways that are being developed come not from institutions, but rather from movements that are more free-form and capture the imagination, especially of the young. These run a spectrum from left to right in terms of their stances toward the established church, but they all have three characteristics in common. First, they have an intense sense of community. Second, they try to give clear form to life, a way to live. In them, ways of living often will take precedence over ways of believing. This intensifies the sense of community. Third, they call for particular sorts of action. So you get movements like the Thomas Community in Finland, like Focolore, Communion and Liberation all the way to Opus Dei and the Legionaries of Christ on the right.

A second strategic pathway that people are choosing is apologetics: trying to interpret the current world and the Christian worldview as a part of that. Reformed theologians, most of whom aren't known here in the English-speaking world, have been trying to reinterpret the world something like the way that Paul Tillich did using existentialist models in the 1950s. The Dominican Study Center has developed a number of little booklets trying to interpret the world in that way.

The third strategic pathway that has emerged has tried to recast Christian teaching in language that's intelligible. I think it's important, in terms of the Catholic perspective on this, to keep a number of things in mind. Three points appear in the U.S. bishops' statements suggesting that the Catholic view of reality has to be a little different from the Reformed one. First, it's much more sacramental, seeing the action of God in the world and not so much perhaps God over against the world. Second, an element that it shares with the Reformed approach, is the centrality of Christ. Third is the importance of narrative, because narratives are how people construct their identities. If we tell stories, if we talk about our families, we describe them with adjectives for a while, but we'll eventually tell representative stories about eccentric uncles, benevolent grandparents, or black sheep that reveal the narrative secrets.

Let me conclude with a word about where I find myself in all of this discussion of pathways. I think of the importance of paradox, of seeing two things going on at the same time. I appreciate paradox very much. It was September 11 that brought this home on this continent in a particular way. It is paradox that the most powerful country in the world, political scientists are saying probably the most powerful military presence the world has ever known, could be undone by a group of young men who took the symbols of our power and crashed one into the other. What that unleashed was an acute sense of vulnerability. Security is the most important need we have after physical survival. Typical of the ethnocentrism of the United States, we say, "September 11 changed the world." Well, it did to a small degree, but it really changed the United States. I think the reason paradox is so important is that it carries tremendous power of interruption, breaking through that veneer that we construct for ourselves of a happy, secure, and safe life. What does that mean for preaching the gospel? I think that an important part of evangelical witness has been social reconciliation. There are elements of reconciliation, healing, and forgiveness that are coming to the forefront for many people that were not the case before. Reconciliation is coming forward because people say, "The enormity of what is going on is more than we can handle and bear." There has to be the possibility of something else, and reconciliation, as we understand it as Christians, provides a way of directing a response to those feelings. Reconciliation is first and foremost God's work in our midst. Reconciliation is not conflict management in the sense of skills we learn that resolve things. There is much that is simply too big for us to manage by ourselves, for us to comprehend, let alone solve. We are agents; we are ambassadors for Christ's sake, as Paul says, when he speaks of reconciliation in 2 Corinthians 5. Second, reconciliation is not about getting over where we were and going back to what we had been before. It's about coming to a new place. Third, vocation is a call to action, a call to go out, to carry this reconciliation forward. We need to rediscover contemplative prayer — especially missionaries, who tend to be activists. If we cannot dwell in the presence of God on God's terms, how do we expect to be God's agents in this situation? How do we expect to be able to hear the woundedness, the cries of pain coming out of the wounds of others, if we have not learned how to live with our own wounds? Pathways of a new evangelization have to deal with both the terrain we're traversing and the way we choose to move on that terrain.

Chapter Six

CONSENTING TO KENOSIS

Mission to Secularity

Michael Downey

T HE THEME OF this symposium, sponsored by the Missionary Oblates of Mary Immaculate, brings to mind the late
Jesuit Bernard Lonergan, who was known to have passed the
remark that the church arrives on the scene late and breathless. The principal theme of this symposium, "secularity" or
"secularism," describes the world we inhabit in the West; it is
as ubiquitous as the air we breathe. It is not something "out
there" or "over there" with an address different from ours. Yet
we are arriving late on the scene — and breathless — having
missed so many opportunities to take the gains of secularity
seriously in our sense of mission in and to the world. So busy
have we been decrying secularism and lamenting its excesses
and distortions that we have missed a gift on offer.

As we address secularity in this symposium on mission to
secularity, it is helpful to remember that a Christian sense of
mission can indeed find common cause with much secular
thinking as we begin to discern the contours of the mission
field whose horizon we are only now begin to recognize —
the terrain of religious pluralism, particularly those religious
phenomena that we would lump under the broad umbrella of
fundamentalism.

I suggest at the outset that engaging the mission to secularity in the dialogical spirit in which it can only be fruitfully exercised today is not nearly as daunting a task as is dialogue of any sort with any kind of religious fundamentalism, even when the dialogue is set within the parameters of the same religious tradition.

Because many of the core gains of secularity are quite compatible with the gospel we seek to proclaim in word and in deed, it is my hope to explore an understanding of mission and secularity by taking stock of the gains that secularity has brought us, aware that a far more daunting mission awaits us on the world scene.

I proceed in four steps. First, I shall articulate what is meant by modern secularity, attentive to some of its strengths and weaknesses. Second, I shall set out an understanding of mission in broader terms than those in which it is commonly understood. Third, I shall look to the theological and spiritual resources to help move forward in mission with the gains of secularity, focusing on the kenosis of God in Christ as key. Fourth, I shall suggest that the mission to secularity is one of testifying to the self-emptying love of God, rather than one of evangelization as it is commonly understood.

Secularity

I understand "secularism," "secularity," and the "secular" as applied to society or culture to be capacious, roomy terms. Their meanings are not easy to pin down. When we speak of mission in a highly secular environment, or culture, our assumptions are often that a secular culture or society or environment is hostile or at least at odds with the mission of Christ and the Spirit. Certainly the Parable of the Sower (Luke 8:4ff.) conveys the message that some soil, or environment, is not good ground for the reception and cultivation of the Living Word. But if the culture or society is thought of principally as hostile, does that not put us in a position of constant nay-saying to the world in which we live? Would not such a conception of culture require us to assume a sustained adversarial position? If we say no to the culture in which we live, then we must say a resounding yes to another way of perceiving and being, ourselves becoming embodiments of what we affirm, a yes that is borne out through a witness of actions that testify to the faith and hope that lie within us.

It might, then, be more helpful for us to consider our culture in terms of *mixed* and *ambiguous* reactions to the gospel, rather than as an environment altogether hostile to it. It may be even more accurate to say that we live in a culture that is *indifferent* to the gospel. If this is so, then what is required is a considerably different approach to mission than what is called for if the culture is conceived of as hostile. Further, if we are willing to reckon with the fact that we have, until now, failed in our mission to secularity, that we have neglected to take seriously its contributions to a renewed humanity, then we might have some small chance of still finding common cause and common ground with those secular thinkers who strive for a renewed sense of the human and of the possibilities for authentic human flourishing.

Hostile to the Gospel?

It is far too easy to paint a picture of North America or the Western world in broad strokes of depravity, debauchery, and decadence, a culture completely at odds with the gospel and the Christian churches. More nuance is not merely desirable, but is required, if we are to respond to the gift and the task of mission. What is needed is sharper discernment, more appreciation for light and shadows as well as darkness. How to perceive and pursue the light in a terribly dark age? How to sift wheat from chaff? In the face of certain developments brought about by science and technology, by cultural fragmentation, and by the widening gap between rich and poor, we must always work in concrete ways to makc a plausible message of hope known and heard.

Let me single out four features of our "secular" environment, usually thought of as creating conditions hostile to the gospel, that call us to deeper discernment.

1. A culture of material plenty is positive or neutral and has certain advantages. Abundance may be a blessing from God. But this must be judged in light of the gap between rich and poor, and in view of the fact that today the acquisition of material abundance is driven by a consumerism that impoverishes millions.

2. A culture of opportunity, with a strong affirmation of individual rights and liberties, is not negative per se. But the unbridled individualism and opportunism in some cultural currents undermines the importance of solidarity cogently articulated by John Paul II[1] and works at cross-purposes with the pursuit of the common good.

3. A culture with a strong commitment to safeguard the freedom of the human person is a good. But where the rhetoric of freedom of choice has muted the rhetoric of commitment to, and responsibility for, others, there must be greater constructive critique and reasoned debate on the part of those who engage in mission to secularity.

4. Tolerance, democratic process, consultation, participation, and accountability are values, even when they cause tension, and at times conflict, with the "culture" of the church. They cannot be dismissed outright as hostile to the gospel, even though at times they manifest themselves as suspicion of authority of any sort, reluctance to give obedience to anyone, or reticence in the face of any claims to truth or universal norms.

These and other features of our culture call for greater discernment. But there are two elements that are clearly antithetical to the gospel. Rather than seeing these as necessarily caused by modern secularism, it would be truer to recognize them as distortions or excesses of secularity. The first is the low esteem for human life increasingly apparent in our culture. This is greatly at odds with the riches of the Christian heritage. If not outright hostile, our culture is certainly "unwelcoming soil" for a Word of Life that safeguards the dignity of each human person created in the image of God, a Word in defense of the wounded and the weak, the last, the littlest and the least.

The second element that creates unwelcoming soil is materialistic consumerism. Pope John Paul II likens its effects to the results of Marxism, Nazism, and Fascism, as well as to the effects of such myths as racial superiority, nationalism, and ethnic exclusivism. *"No less pernicious* [emphasis mine], though not always as obvious, are the effects of materialistic consumerism, in which the exaltation of the individual and the selfish satisfaction of personal aspirations become the ultimate goal of life."[2]

Mission to secularity entails a mature response to the truth that, even with the losses that secularism has brought, the secular mind-set has also brought true gains. These gains of modern secularity might be articulated crisply as follows:

1. the person matters and has choices;

2. the person has inherent rights and liberties, which today would include the right to education, to employment, and to health care;

3. the person has the freedom to choose religion and is to be free from religious constraint;

4. the person has the freedom of inquiry, the intellectual freedom to explore the humanities, the sciences, in the various spheres of life;

5. the "other" exists and does matter;

6. people have a voice and it matters;

7. the truth cannot be put forward as true solely on the basis of authority.

Even though the rhetoric of choice may have eclipsed the rhetoric of commitment, and even though modern secularism has failed to make good on its promise to establish a new foundation for human flourishing within the human in and of itself, who would be willing to jettison these hard-earned gains brought by the advent of modern secularity?

Finally, and perhaps above all, it must be noted that secularism or secularity does not necessarily mean the eclipse of the holy or the death of the sacred, but the relocation of the foundation for discussing both within the human. The secularist spiritual humanism of the French philosopher Luc Ferry[3] or the "half belief" of Italian philosopher Gianni Vattimo[4] give ample evidence of an acknowledgment of the dignity of the person, concern for the common good, a sentiment for life as a gift in such terms as "sacrifice," "agape," and "solidarity" — all in a decidedly secular key that strikes harmony with the rhythm of the Word and the Spirit in whose mission the baptized participate.

Mission

Mission is not just one dimension or element of the church. It is not so much that the church has a mission; it is rather more that the mission has a church. What is this mission? It is none other than that of Jesus Christ the Word, and of the Holy Spirit, the gift of God's love dwelling in our hearts.

Jesus' mission is to announce the time of God's favor, the coming of the reign of God. Jesus proclaimed the reign of God as the fulfillment of God's hope, desire, and intention for the world now and to come. In God's Reign, truth, holiness, justice, love, and peace will hold sway forever. Jesus established the church to continue and further this mission. He entrusted *this* mission to the church: to proclaim in word and deed the good news of God's coming among us in Jesus Christ through the gift of the Spirit. This mission is so central to the word and work of Jesus that the Second Vatican Council affirmed and emphasized that "mission" defines the church. The church in every dimension of its life and practice exists for mission: to proclaim in word and deed the reign of God to people in every culture, time, and place.

Through Christian baptism, we participate in the life and mission of Word and Spirit. This mission is manifest in the theophany at the river Jordan. Jesus is named Son by the Father in the Spirit. But in this very naming, the Son is the one sent, impelled by the Spirit to be tempted by the devil and to combat evil. He preaches the reign of God, announces the good news that in the time of God's favor the oppressed are set free, the blind see. Indeed in his words and in his work, Jesus embodies God's intention for the world now and to come, a world transfigured in and by love. His life was not a free and easy ride, but a continual struggle against injustice and hate, illness, suffering, and depersonalization. The reign of God, God's intention for the world now and to come, is realized only in a communion in the one Love, which he manifests most fully at the table on the night before he died and in his self-giving on the cross, anticipated in his Transfiguration on Mount Tabor (Matt. 17:1–8; Mark 9:2–8; Luke 9:28–36; 2 Pet. 1:16–18).

Word and Spirit are made manifest, thereby inviting our active participation in the mission through which the world is transformed by love itself into a communion in love. At once sent forth and carried by the mission of Word and Spirit, it is our gift and task to participate in love's creative and animating activity in the world. Who we are as persons is realized in bringing forth God's love and in all creative expressions of love. It is ours to live in the flow of divine life in the mission of Christ and Spirit — moving into deeper communion with the source and end of love itself.

Word is love heard and seen. Spirit is the principle of love's creativity and bonding. In the Son and the Holy Spirit, God is speaking and breathing. Word is what is said; Spirit is the saying. What is said in the saying is Love itself. But love expressed and bonding takes many different forms. To participate in the mission of Word and Spirit is to see and to share in the manifold manifestations of human expressivity and creativity as they disclose the divine reality. The Christian call is to flow with and in the missions of Word as expressivity and Spirit as creativity, communicating and bringing forth the one Love. In human expressivity and in various configurations of human creativity and bonding we come to know something of the magnitude of the God who is love. Our gift and task in mission is to cultivate, nurture, and sustain the great variety of the manifestations of the magnitude of God's love in all forms of expressivity and creativity. For human life and destiny are realized not in the exercise of individual rights and liberties, but in all those creative expressions of love that lead to a fuller communion in the one Love itself.

Participation in the mission of Word and Spirit thus understood subverts commonly held understandings of mission and evangelization.

Such a view of mission does not mean "selling Jesus" in the marketplace, "dumbing down" the gospel, or making it more palatable to the "spiritually hungry" in our consumerist culture. If we are to persuade others of the veracity of the claims we make, and not make facile appeals to authority as the basis for the faith and hope in us, then we must ourselves be persuaded of the plausibility of our claims as borne out in the testimony of our lives lived in and through love.

Theological and Spiritual Resources for Mission to Secularity

What are the theological resources that we have to help us move forward in mission to secularity, cognizant of the fact that another mission yet awaits us? How might these resources serve not only the mission to secularity, but the emergent sense of mission on a religiously pluralistic and increasingly fundamentalist world scene?

As we take stock of our gains, we must also lament what has been lost in the process of secularization. We need to learn from the theological and spiritual heritage of our forebears among the people of Israel who weep and wail "Why?" before God's face. Lament is not endless moaning, but springs from the hard recognition of deep loss that gives way to hope. And the losses brought on by the advent of secularity have not been small.

My suggestion is that the richest theological resource we have in the tradition, in addition to lament giving rise to hope, is that of an understanding of the gift/ing God disclosed in the kenosis. At this juncture, the central question might be framed this way: Who is this Christ we seek to proclaim, be it to the secular world or to those of different religious traditions, fundamentalist or other?

In *Fides et Ratio,* John Paul II spells out what he sees as the "current tasks for theology."[5] He writes: "The very heart of theological inquiry will thus be the contemplation of the mystery of the Triune God."[6] Further, "From this vantage point, the prime commitment of theology is seen to be the understanding of God's kenosis, a grand and mysterious truth for the human mind, which finds it inconceivable that suffering and death can express a love which gives itself and seeks nothing in return."[7] In line with Hans Urs van Balthasar, John Paul II maintains that the prime task of theology is "understanding God's kenosis" and, by implication, that the Kenotic Christ, the self-emptying of God in Christ, the divine self-abandon, is the most apt Christological image for our own day.

It is my suggestion that this understanding is most apt not only for theology, but also for every dimension of the church's life. But what does God's kenosis mean? And why is seeking to understand this mystery apposite for the church's mission? Seeking to answer this question is not only a response to John Paul II's challenge to understand God's kenosis. It is also to ponder the very purpose of mission in a way that leads to the contemplation of the mystery of the Triune God.[8]

To speak of the kenosis is to speak of the Incarnation of God in Christ. It is nothing more, or less, than the mystery of Christ's identification with the human reality. But with a particular slant, informed by a singular insight. And the insight is that of self-emptying, best understood in light of Philippians 2 and 1 Corinthians 1, which contrasts human wisdom and the folly of the cross.

From the vantage point of kenosis, God comes without pretension, in contrast to our highly pragmatic, utilitarian approaches to mission, often rooted in our inordinate desire to achieve. The kenosis puts a question to any and all systems of thought. The divine mystery does not rest in some sense of God's inscrutability, but rather in the truth that God should appear in such a fashion. Kenosis is the scene on which God appears, refusing to identify with human achievement, resisting the inordinate need, or demand, to measure success, to assess projected outcomes. All these defy the logic of the gift, the emptying out of self in order to appear on that scene, the scene of human weakness and vulnerability, to identify with human beings in the concrete circumstances of their lives. This is a God who does not fill in for human want, but is present *amidst* it, *amidst* human longing and want. This is the meaning of God's kenosis.

Who is the Christ we proclaim in word and deed in mission? From the vantage of kenosis God is the God of self emptying love. The God whose very life is the Love that pours itself forth in divine self-abandon. This changes what we understand mission to be: We go empty-handed as those who share in the self-emptying of God in Christ.

Mission is itself a participation in the kenosis. The further I follow in this way of mission of Word and Spirit, the more I must accept the provisionality of all I know and say and do. One of the most important things in life is learning how not to know. This is not the same as simply not knowing. What is meant by "not to know" here involves admitting, accepting, and embracing our limits. This involves embracing the tensive interaction between knowing and not knowing: to recognize our own emptiness so as to receive the gift of wisdom on offer. Even from secular thinkers.

Engaging in mission to secularity is to see, to read, to contemplate the presence of God in the unlikely places. God does not fill in the gaps, or take away human want, or serve as a stopgap when we fail in our otherwise quite effective missionary efforts — at least according to our standards of assessment. God is present, even and especially amid the failure of our best-intentioned efforts. How far do we follow Christ in the admission that in so many ways we have failed to announce the gospel of Christ in a way that truly gives life? To the ends, edges, borders, limits of a church that is now being called to willingly consent to the self-emptying of God *and the self-emptying of the church,* so that a new understanding of mission and a new approach to mission can come into being by the gift of the gift/ing God — not by our own well-intentioned and quite earnest efforts at mission.

Kenosis: Key to Mission

With kenosis as key, we must take up mission anew, in the spirit of a new evangelization that is truly new in its methods, expression, and zeal.[9] Taking up the mission to secularity in this spirit of kenosis gives us our only hope. But with this gift comes judgment. The counterpart of hope is the admission of shortcomings, indeed of failure, despite our noblest intentions. Such an admission makes room for the Spirit's gift/ing in hope. Indeed hope of the deepest kind calls for humility, a willingness to be judged by the gospel, to submit to its apocalyptic sting. May I suggest, however, that it is not simply our culture that needs to be judged by the Lordship of Christ? At times it is also our own exercise of mission. For many people both inside and outside the church, we have not provided reasons for hope, but ample reasons for indifference and, at times, hostility. To acknowledge this is a necessary step in responding with a full heart to the challenge of mission to secularity.

The Parable of the Sower conveys a message about different kinds of soil, or environments, for the Word. Because some of these are indifferent or hostile to sowing the seed of God's Word does not absolve us of the effort to sow continually. The parable offers a message of hope to all — especially those involved in spreading words and planting seeds — not to be discouraged. If hope in Christ gives any assurance it is this: the more unpropitious the circumstances, the greater the challenge to hope.

What are the habits, attitudes, dispositions that emerge from cultivating a deep and abiding awareness of the kenosis of God in Christ in the church as the key to mission?

Above all, we go with empty hands, willing to receive the gift on offer in the other, even and especially those we are inclined to call "godless." This entails a willingness to listen. *Listening* is a discipline. It is a necessary form of asceticism if mission is to be fruitful. Today there seems to be a short supply of people who are schooled in its practice. And people everywhere seem short on patience. Many in our day have lost the knack for following a line of thinking to its conclusion, or staying the course of a conversation until completion. We are unable to really hear another, so often because our mind is galloping toward what we think we should say in response.

Additionally, there is need for a greater measure of tolerance, a *profound respect* for those who are different from ourselves. Not only can we be intolerant of the perspectives or positions of others, we can also find the sometimes very painful process of patient listening to be utterly intolerable. We may find ourselves appealing to authority to bring an end to the conversation. We may be inclined to "close the question" when what might be called for is yet more patient, disciplined listening.

In the practice of listening, it is sometimes better to say nothing in the way of response. It is often in silence and receptivity that we are able to hear the Word beneath and beyond the words of those whose voice we would rather not hear.

If we are to listen patiently, we must accept that there are no quick results and few, if any, easy answers to the highly complex issues facing us. We must develop the habit of listening long enough to hear the "question behind the question," to discern the "issue beneath the issue" on an agenda. We often use the same or similar words when it comes to matters of gospel faith and life, but we may mean quite different things.

This may give rise to a crucial question for those entrusted with the mission: How do I react, or respond, to difference? How do I relate to those who disagree with me? For our mission to be good news, we need to cultivate and sustain a balanced disposition marked by genuine respect for others, even the enemy. To the degree that we are able, we ought to seek to be impartial and unselfish, willing to relinquish what the truth demands of us. When there is openness and willingness to listen in a spirit of respect and charity, when there is humility in the face of the truth, this may require of us "a review of assertions and attitudes."[10]

But alongside respect for the differences of others, we need a hefty measure of *confidence*. We must be confident not only in the integrity and plausibility of our own convictions, but confident as well in the good will and integrity of those whose life-world is secular through and through. If we are suspicious or unsure of the motives of others, or so overly confident in the plausibility of our positions as to think that they are above scrutiny, then we may be unable to engage in mission in a manner which is, in itself, a proclamation of good news.

In the face of indifference, mission is to be exercised in a spirit of *humility*, another virtue that seems in short supply in our day. Humility does not take offense, nor does it offend. It is not at home with rancor or bitterness. It does not demand having its own way. It is not smug or self-reliant. Rather, humility is expressed in healthy self-effacement, a willingness to listen — even when those in the secular world or in the culture-at-large make claims that we would rather not hear. Humility is expressed in the avoidance of peremptory language, in tranquility, in patience under contradiction, in gentleness, in generosity of spirit. Along with respect for difference, patient listening, and confidence, humility is a sine qua non of mission in a secular world, in an environment indifferent to the gospel.

Our Mission: To Testify

The recognition of our failure in the mission to secularity is a deep summons to repentance and reconciliation. This entails not only recognizing our failure vis-à-vis secularity, but just as much, if not more, an admission of the way we have failed in our exercise of mission in past epochs. Part of our mission today is to testify, through humble gestures of repentance, that at certain moments in history our mission has brought with it the suppression of peoples, colonization, the eradication of cultures and traditional religious beliefs among peoples. Indeed the emergence of modern secularism has helped to serve as a corrective to many forms of religious domination, and for this we should give thanks.

If the "new evangelization" proposed by Pope John Paul II is to be really *new* — new in its expression, its methods, its zeal, then it must be grounded in the "purification of memories"[11] to which we are summoned, calling upon persons and groups to forgive us for the evil and the harm that we have inflicted in the name of Christ and the gospel. Now is the acceptable time to admit that we may not have been as effective at evangelization as we might have been, and to recognize our need for forgiveness for those times when our mission took the form of Western and European domination of indigenous cultures rather than a true proclamation of good news.

Too often, approaches to mission have been impelled by a governing concern for "sacramentalization" rather than evangelization. Moreover, we have often been inclined to think that because we have taught we have evangelized. Even today, teaching on matters of doctrine and morality does not sufficiently take into account the fact that people do not automatically receive this teaching as good news. How do we help people of many different "cultures" who are listening to us — sometimes all at once — hear the gospel as good news? Only if they see in our lives a testimony to the self-emptying love of God known in the kenosis of Christ.

Do others know us to be people who have had a fresh "encounter with the Lord,"[12] the Lord of Lords and King of Kings whose very life is self-emptying love? Does this encounter manifest itself in a witness of actions, a testimony of life?

One of the central challenges of the gospel is to make the values of the reign of God our own — holiness, truth, justice, love, and peace — and then to live them out in the midst of a world that does not choose or even value them, sometimes swimming against the tide. But even as we do so, our first task in mission is not to correct and chide, but to remain approachable and open, collaborative and supportive of all who truly seek common cause and common good.

It is a very simplistic reading of a complex situation to say that indifference or hostility to the gospel is the result of deeply embedded cultural factors. Could it be rather that many are indifferent to the church and its mission because the saving message of the gospel has not been taught in a way that really *gives life*, in a way that helps people make sense out of their lives and loves, inviting and encouraging them to live in this dark age with just a bit more hope and a clearer sense of future?

We often rely on words that are familiar to people whose faith has been cultivated, nurtured and sustained in a Christian or specifically Catholic culture — the language of sin, grace, salvation, redemption, resurrection. But do we speak this language in a way that helps others comprehend the meaning of our words? How might the rhetoric of our proclamation ring out as good news to those who are actually poor and homeless, to the single parent, to a young person with a chronic illness?

Our mission must hold out a promise of life in face of the reality of evil and sin, to be sure. But, just as much, it should help people live the joys and delights of human life in the presence of the divine, to see and to celebrate all that they have as gift through and through. If we see the task of mission as the imparting of doctrine, however subtle, or of conversion to a particular religious confession, rather than as speaking a Word of Life, then our words will likely be semantically empty, lacking real meaning for those in a secular world. Unless we rise to the challenge of passing on a Word that gives life through testimony, it should come as no surprise not only that those in modern secular culture remain indifferent, but also that those within the church grow increasingly indifferent.

We are not true to the mission of Word and Spirit amid secularity when we appeal to religious authority, be it scriptural or magisterial, as the basis and rationale of our message. Much more is required if our words are to be a Word of Life in unwelcoming soil. In the face of indifference, the hope for effective mission rests in presenting an argument that is persuasive of the message. But the argument must be borne out in our personal witness to the truth we seek to proclaim, in witness of action, in testimony. If the culture is thought to be hostile to the gospel, we may be inclined to think that a firm hand or a sharp voice is the proper strategy. But if the culture is just plain indifferent, then the only chance of getting through is with a message at once precise and persuasive, rooted in a personal praxis of the gospel.

Recall the words of Pope Paul VI: "Modern man listens more willingly to witnesses than to teachers, and if he does listen to teachers, it is because they are witnesses."[13]

The Testimony

To what do we testify? To what do we bear witness in mission? In the mission of Word and Spirit we participate in the life of the divine Trinity. The doctrine of the Trinity affirms that God is immutably turned toward us and for us in self-giving love, that the very being of God is constituted by the self-giving that is constitutive of love. God is not self-enclosed or self-contained, but toward us, for us, with us, and in us. God is Giver, Given, and Gift/ing. To claim that God is love (1 John 4:8) is to say that God is the life that pours itself forth, always, everywhere, unceasingly, never-to-stop coming as gift. God is love in the way that a ruby is red or an emerald green. God's love is such that it is never emptied but is, rather, all the fuller in the giving of it. This is the wisdom of the Kenotic Christ, emptied in self-gift from crib to table to cross.

Who is God? The mystery of God's kenosis discloses a God who is ad-vent-ing. The God disclosed in Christ's kenosis is the God who comes and is coming. To contemplate the mystery of the Triune God from this vantage point is to see that human life, history, the world, and the church, even and especially in all their brokenness and vulnerabilty, have been seized and saturated by gift. But such a way of seeing is itself a gift given only when we are willing to set aside the "wisdom of the world" and embrace the "folly of the cross." This is a language and a logic of gift, which many others are seeking to speak and to live by, even some of those who are unrepentantly secular.

Who is the Christ whose gospel we are seeking to bring to a secular culture by our testimony? I suggest that it is the one who emptied himself and took the form of a slave. His Lordship is that of slave, outcast, servant. To this we witness and to this we testify in word and deed, by willingly consenting to kenosis in our life and in our mission. But at this point in our history the church is resisting, rather than consenting, to the self-emptying to which it is being invited. Talk of purification is not so much about the deep purification of memories to which we are summoned — for our failures and neglect in mission, and for the harm that we have brought to persons, peoples, and cultures in the name of Christ and gospel. So much talk of purification in the church today is aimed at catharsis, cleansing, so that we can return to the scene, pure and strong again to — dare I say it — pick up where we left off before these interruptions brought on by "the scandal" and by the erosion of the faith caused by secularism. Such a purification can easily bypass the call to the deepest kind of forgiveness and reconciliation that is needed, without which the church — not just individuals within it — continues in the way of evil and sin. If the church has a mission to secularity, it begins anew each day by asking forgiveness, even and especially from "godless people" and "godless nations," present and past.

Whether it be to secularity or to those of other religious traditions — be they fundamentalist or those of the more critically conscious kind — our mission is one that recognizes the kenosis of God in Christ as the *movement of God in our own time and place.* It does not resist, but enters into the kenosis especially as it is manifest *in the emptying of the church,* in the splintering of its structures, the demise of its institutions, its diminishing influence on the world scene, the shrinking of numbers of its clergy and vowed religious. The testimony does not hearken back to some golden age of Christian history, or look to the day when our numbers will be greater and our institutions stronger. The testimony to God's love takes the form of *freely consenting to emptying — even of what we thought mission to be — as a participation in the divine life.* And then, in bold testimony to the hope that lies within us, to be willing to attend to the gift on offer, a gift for the life of the world, being spoken by those who are seeking and finding the traces of the holy in vastly different ways, in this world and no other.

Notes

1. See, for example, his encyclicals *Laborem exercens* (1981), 9ff., and *Sollicitudo rei socialis* (1987), 38ff.

2. John Paul II, Message for the Celebration of the World Day of Peace, January 1, 1999, "Respect for Human Rights: The Secret of True Peace," 2.

3. Luc Ferry, *Man Made God: The Meaning of Life*, trans. David Pellauer (Chicago: University of Chicago Press, 2002).

4. Gianni Vattimo, *Belief*, trans. David Webb and Luca D'Isanto (Stanford, CA: Stanford University Press, 2000).

5. *Fides et Ratio* (1998), 92–99.

6. Ibid., 93.

7. Ibid.

8. Ibid.

9. For John Paul II's view of evangelization see his Post-Synodal Apostolic Exhortation *Ecclesia in America* (January 22, 1999), 6, 28, and 66, *AAS* 91 (1999): 737–815; Apostolic Letter *Tertio Millennio Adveniente* (November 10, 1994), 21, *AAS* 87 (1995): 17; Address at the Opening of the Fourth General Conference of Latin American Bishops (October 12, 1992), 17, *AAS* 85 (1993): 820; Encyclical *Redemptoris Missio* (December 7, 1990), 37, *AAS* 83 (1991): 249–340; Post-Synodal Exhortation *Christifideles Laici* (December 30, 1988), 34, *AAS* 81 (1989): 455.

10. John Paul II, *Ut unum sint* (1995), 36.

11. The call to purification of memories was clearly elicited in John Paul II's various writings in preparation for the Great Jubilee 2000. He reiterates this need as he articulates his vision for the new millennium in his Apostolic Letter *Novo Millennio Ineunte* (2001), 6.

12. John Paul II, Apostolic Exhortation *Ecclesia in America* (1999), 4.

13. My translation from the French. See Pope Paul VI, "Address to the Members of the *Consilio de Laicis*" (October 2, 1974), *AAS* 66 (1974): 568.

Chapter Seven

NAMING THE CONTEXT OF NORTH AMERICA

Where Is Here? How Is Now?

Mary Jo Leddy

I T IS A RISKY BUSINESS to try to assess the times one lives in, the place and the culture called home in the world. It remains forever a provisional task, fraught with the constant possibility of misreading, misconstruing the signs of the times. Hindsight or a certain detachment of mind seems to make things clearer. Nevertheless, it may be even more risky to avoid the challenge of naming the direction of the current of one's own time. There is the danger of going with the flow, of preaching fidelity from a sinking ship while the people are looking for a lifeboat. "Where are we going?" they cry. "Why are we swimming? Is there another way?"

Like fish in the water, it is difficult for us to know the culture we swim in. I sometimes envy missionaries who are sent to another place, not here. Most know that they must make some effort to understand a culture that is different and strange. But what are we to make of the familiar and the friendly? Of the thick and the thinness of it all? All too often, it seems just like reality, like normal. This is especially true if we live within the most dominant culture in the world — which, for want of better terms, I will call America, the north and the west. (A word to the Canadians here: I assume we are

at least a colony in this culture. Since September 11 we are
quietly being transformed into a state of America.)

This conference is important in that it intentionally seeks
to take a second look at the culture which has, in many ways,
given us the ability to see. We must *see through*, a term that I
am using deliberately because of its double connotation — to
see below the surface of things, to feel the deeper current of
our times *and* to see through in the sense of being committed
in a responsible way. If we are not willing to lift the sandbags,
if we do not care about the people on the shore, we will not
see the floodwaters as they rise. Consciousness is intimately
linked to commitment and care. Do we care enough about
our people to think deeply, to speak truthfully, to name the
present moment?

Perspectives on the Present

The Wisdom of the Crucified

I assume this as a starting point: Where you live determines
what you see. The people you listen to influence what you
hear. And so I must begin with giving you a little more detail
about where I live and whom I listen to in the course of my
daily life. Romero House is actually four houses and a store-
front center in a little pie-shaped, no-name neighborhood in
the west end of Toronto. In each house we have political
refugees from all over the world and others, like myself, who
live with them and work for them. We welcome strangers and
live with them as neighbors, trying to love them as ourselves.
This welcome is extended by full-time live-in younger people,
called interns, who give a year or more of their lives to this
service.

Through the refugees who have become my neighbors, I
have learned to see my own culture, my own backyard, with
new eyes.

These strangers, these outsiders, are the eyes of my eyes, the ears of my ears. They have come to this continent seeking refuge, trusting in what is best in our culture, trusting in the respect for human rights that we have promised to uphold. But they have also come here because of the shadow side of America, the north and the west. Their countries have been torn apart by cold war conflicts that have persisted in new forms as the armies of the East and West packed their bags and went home. They come from places where tribal conflicts have been fueled by the craving of the West for things like oil, like diamonds. These strangers know that we are better than we think and worse than we know.

However, they say little about all of this. They would prefer to remain silent (knowing the high cost of speaking the truth) and would like to become invisible. As I have lived with such as these for almost twelve years now, I have assumed my place with Mary at the foot of their cross. Waiting, witnessing the dying, listening for signs of life, hoping against hope, knowing that, although there are things I can and must do, there is little I can do to take away their immense loneliness and suffering.

I have come to understand that theirs is a crucified wisdom. Like that of millions of people throughout the world, their suffering is not only unheard, it is mute — unable to speak, unheard amid the white noise of the airwaves. Only occasionally do they speak a word that is heard and recorded. "I thirst." "Why have you abandoned me?" It is the people at the foot of the cross who must take those words to heart, so that the crucified are not reduced to yet another sound bite of suffering. It is in their bodies that they bear the truth about the burden of these times: scarred, tortured, raped.

When we look upon the face of a crucified one, we are (as Emanuel Levinas says) faced. We see not a refined icon but a naked and vulnerable face, an icon that has been defaced, a face that summons and commands: you must think about me, about us, about the systems and the cultures that will not look upon us — and be saved.

As it was two thousand years ago, the crucified ones reveal the truth of the culture that is worse than we know. These refugees are not the only crucified ones. Thousands of others fill our cities, in the alleys and on the sidewalks. They may chatter and rave, but they are seldom heard. There are others, in the suburbs who feel like yelling but catch themselves, because, well, we have so much — like the female real estate agent in *American Beauty*.

Yet these crucified ones also reveal that we as a culture are better than we know. Not all of the refugees who come to our homes are Christians. In fact, there have been years when I was the only Christian in my house; most of the others were Muslim. Yet it is these people who have shocked me into wonder once again about what is really *good* about the "good news." For many of them it is the first time in which they experienced that they would be treated with complete respect, offered affection, regardless of their tribal origin or religious commitment. "Neither Jew nor Greek," "slave nor free," "male nor female." It is the first time in which someone has given them something — for nothing. It is an overwhelming experience for them and a completely reconstituting experience for those of use who have grown all too accustomed to the gospel words.

The Perspective of Future Generations

The people I listen to are also the young college students (from the United States, Canada, and from all over the world) who come as interns to Romero House. My experience with them confirms much of what John Shea and Robert Schreiter have said in this conference. These young people are spiritually interested but, in general, religiously illiterate.

These young people are given a great deal of responsibility; they live side by side with people who have gone through a dark night that is at least spiritual. They have tea and listen to people who have to sift and sort what is left of their lives, who have to reassess what really matters. They watch people who have nothing celebrate as if they had everything. The need for a sustainable spirituality quickly becomes evident.

Because of the chaotic nature of our work and the depth of suffering we encounter, we have structured our day to provide points of reference and community. There are regular meals, regular times for leisure, regular times of prayer and liturgy that follow the traditional Catholic practices. We say the psalms together and follow the lectionary of the day. All the good will that our interns bring is channeled through a certain discipline, practices for the long haul. Most of the interns find these practices immensely helpful and even energizing. Note that many of them have never had regular meals or regular anything in their families. These are the generation of grazers, who browse around in refrigerators when they feel hungry. They love being with other young adults who don't think they are crazy for caring and hoping and believing. They begin to see and imagine the world in a different way, through the images of scripture that they hear every day — of a world in which there is happiness in giving, a world in which there is a love beyond death, a world in which goodness matters more than greatness. A world in which they matter.

They begin to see and hear the world through different eyes and ears, through the eyes and ears of the crucified ones. Their sense of priorities begins to shift.

Most of these interns were able to participate in the World Youth Day that was held recently in Toronto, and we were able to host young people from around the world. It was a marvelous experience of community, of the world Catholic community for them. They saw themselves not only as part of the global suffering but as part of the global hope.

In fact, there were relatively few young people from Toronto at the World Youth Day. Some of this had to do with organizational problems at the local level, some of it had to do with the regrettable decision to appeal for participation through the parishes rather than the Catholic high schools. But a great deal of it had to do with the ho-hum attitude of the secular culture. However, what did summon many young people (and even reluctant Catholics) away from the TV set and toward the large papal Mass was the sight of the pope as he walked down the long steps from the airplane to the tarmac. The word had been that he was too sick to travel, too weak to walk, too wracked with pain to manage the steps on his own. A crane of sorts was to lower him down.

What happened when the plane landed was a sight to behold. Slowly, deliberately, painfully, he walked down those steps on his own. When our interns saw this they said: He has made such an effort to come and see us. We matter to him. Now we will make an effort to greet him. His actions gave weight to his words. That's what counted for these young people. They know that words are cheap. They know, better than we think, the difference between image and reality. When someone is real, when his or her actions give weight to the image, that is tremendously compelling and convincing.

During those five days in July, the pope said very little about the church (although he did make a clear statement about the shame of the church regarding the abuse scandals). His message was much more to the heart of the matter. He said to the young people, "You matter. You can make a difference in the world. You face a great moral challenge that is worthy of your lives."

Conservative Catholics had hoped for a little more about the church. So had the liberal Catholics, who wanted the pope to speak more about the issues in the church that seemed so important: greater democracy and transparency, the ordination of women, the acceptance of homosexuality, etc. Some liberal commentators even said that the young people at the WYD had been duped, that if they really knew what was going on in the church, they wouldn't be so captivated by the pope.

It was an arrogant assessment of the younger generation (and it confirms Robert Schreiter's remarks on the attitudes of different generations toward the church). In fact, these kids (at least the ones I had talked to) had heard a great deal about the sex abuse scandals and had even grown up hearing their parents' criticisms of the church. It wasn't that they didn't know what was going on, it just seemed less important than the words they longed to hear: *Your lives are important. You have something to give to the world, and it matters that you give it.* They heard the words from someone whose life gave weight to his words.

This is where my insight into the present moment is located, where it begins. It begins to name the moment where our local realities are connected with the suffering and hope of wider global movements. And sustaining those connections involves much more than a vague spiritual sense of connectedness but the real human connections that are called church.

However, every insight has its oversights. There are other eyes and ears on the present moment that I must attend to as well.

Perspective of Insiders Who Are Outsiders

I take the refugees to be outsiders who are now inside our culture — and who thus provide a critical and creative distance from the dominant culture. However, there are also insiders who are outsiders — those who live with an alternative vision to the dominant culture: the contemplatives, the artists, and those who have lived in other cultures and who have returned to North America — people like returning missionaries.

My own assessment is that the contemplative tradition is alive and well in North America and that if one were to draw the contours of the living church (the living, breathing church) it would consist of dots across the continent, and those dots would be renewal centers, retreat houses, monasteries where weary nomads come in search of living water. This is the geography of the spirit in this time and in this place. Of course there are some wacky places, but most of them are forms of a parallel culture where alternatives to the dominant culture are being nourished and being kept alive. I leave it to you to tell us what you see when you return to America, the north and the west.

Then there are the artists who can imagine the worst and the best of a culture. (By artists I mean writers, poets, playwrights, musicians, etc.) I hang out with some of these people, and I know that there are some who are more interested in an artistic lifestyle than in life. However, I have met enough true artists to value what they see and hear, and I think I have some understanding of why they are so important in the process of naming a reality that we barely know and can hardly articulate. Artists name through images, symbols, and stories. Their questions about a culture are already bridges to their own answers.

Naming the Present as an Act of Imagination

Let me say something very briefly about the correlation between the artistic imagination of a culture and the imaginative construal of reality that is found in the scriptures. It is the process of correlation that can take place within an individual or, more appropriately, within a community.

I do not think that the artists (or the philosophers and thinkers) articulate the questions of a culture, which are then opened to the answers of scripture. I suspect it goes something more like this: a person or community internalizes the symbols and narratives of scripture to the point where they begin to transform the deepest levels of imagination. This is much easier said than done in a culture saturated with images. It involves a constant, daily reference to the scriptures — a pondering, a praying, a saying, and a singing until they transform the unconscious level of a person or community. It involves a biblical imagination.

If this person or community then internalizes the symbols and images of a culture, beyond and below the level of consciousness, then those two sets of images meet, collide, conflict, or cohere. The sifting and sorting take place, I believe, largely on an unconscious level, and it is difficult to distinguish the source of imaginative breakthrough. Yet there does arise in consciousness the moment when an image or name seems to "fit" the reality of one's own time and place. From that pre-reflective meeting of images (from the scripture and from the culture) there may issue forth a naming, an intuition, an insight — call it what you will. A name that rings out anew words like "temptation," "idolatry," "salvation," and "redemption." It then falls to the theologian to see whether and how such a name can become the source of further reflection. The symbol gives rise to thought, as Paul Ricoeur says. It then belongs to the community of faith to discern if this is a true naming. I sometimes think that the most important reason people like myself must write our thoughts down is that we must give them over to the community to see if they are worthy and appropriate.

Imagining the Present Moment

With this in mind, I want to explore how three works of art have named the present moment: the film *American Beauty*, the film *The Decline of the American Empire*, and the novel *Underworld* by Don DeLillo.

American Beauty is a searing depiction of the misery of the life of a very materialistic middle-class family in the suburbs. On the surface the family seems to have everything, but their lives are unhappy and meaningless. Their lives and their relationships are being consumed to the point of nothingness. One of their greatest fears is being ordinary and boring. For a moment, sex seems to offer almost everyone a temporary reprieve from their lives — which are simultaneously frantic and boring. (There is a subtle captivity in this middle-class existence, which I have described [as captivity and liberation] at length in *Radical Gratitude*.) It is the young drug dealer on the block who seems to have some insight into what is missing in this scene. He has made a film of a plastic bag, which is dancing, almost like an angel in the autumn leaves. As he watches this (on film) he says it is as if "there was this entire life behind things and this incredibly benevolent force that wanted me to know there was no reason to be afraid ever. . . . I need to remember. Sometimes there's so much beauty in the world I feel like I can't take it and my heart's just going to cave in."

Toward the end of the film, the father — "just an ordinary guy with nothing to lose" — is killed and, as his life flashes before him, the good moments of his life come to mind. They are very ordinary moments: "the yellow leaves on the maple trees, my grandmother's hands, the first time I saw my cousin Tony's brand-new Firebird. . . . And Janey, and Janey and Carolyn. I can't feel anything but gratitude for every single moment of my stupid little life." The American beauty turns out to be not some teenage cheerleader, but the beauty of the ordinary life, which is recognized in gratitude.

The Decline of the American Empire is the name of the film by Quebec director Denys Arcand. In the opening scene, we hear an articulate and rather jaded academic analyze the present moment for a young radio interviewer. In a time of political decline, says the professor, people cease to invest their energy in a common social project and turn toward more personal projects, such as the development and the fulfillment of the self. Only in a developing culture, she lectures, is there a common social vision compelling enough to invite individuals to transcend their personal interests for the sake of something greater. The rest of the film is an exploration of the cultivation of the self that takes place as a group of academics goes off on a weekend together. One suggestive statement floats out over the water as a voice-over toward the end of the film: "We have no vision, no models or metaphors to live by. Only the saints and the mystics live well at a time like this."

The novel *Underworld* by Don DeLillo is, in my opinion, the finest novel of the decade. If you look at the cover, designed at least two years before the destruction of the World Trade Center, it appears almost prophetic: in the background are the twin towers in New York City and an airplane in flight, and in the foreground is an old church.

The book is a multileveled panorama (jazz, baseball, Jesuit high school, "Long Tall Sally") of American history from 1951 to 1991. It encompasses the period of the cold war, which opened with the explosion of an atomic bomb in the Soviet Union (on the same day that the Giants won the World Series with a ninth-inning homer) and closed with the fall of the Berlin Wall in 1991.

For Don DeLillo, this has been a defining period for America, the time in which it had a great known enemy, the time in which it gradually became more defined by what it was against than what it was for. It was a time of the creation of ever newer weapons, and the by-product is waste. "Waste is the secret history," he writes, "the underhistory" of this time. And so the key character in the story is a waste manager who tries to recycle garbage and his former girlfriend who tries to redeem old Air Force planes by painting them with beautiful colors and designs.

For DeLillo America began to resemble the great terror it had been fighting. The Bronx is presented as the American Gulag filled with garbage, drug addicts, and child prostitutes — who are treated like garbage and who die in the garbage.

In the midst of the garbage stands the church, which resembles nothing so much as the church of the catacombs. Monks and nuns go out with food to the children in the garbage and there they meet Moonwalker, the artist who works with spray paint on the wall. Every time a child dies he paints an angel on the wall. They are remembered and named.

As the book unfolds, all the pieces of the past from what happened in the Bronx on a day in 1951 come together —

it is all connected, the baseball, the weapons, and the waste. Yet the book concludes with a vision of how everything is connected in a vision of peace.

The American Moment and the Summoning of Christianity

I cannot do justice to these profound artistic insights into our culture. However, I do think they all name this present moment as *the American Moment.*

Allow me to elaborate. What is presented is an image of America as an empire. This is an image that does not sit comfortably with many Americans who are steeped in the values and vision of the republic. However, many historians will argue that the transformation of the republic to an empire has happened over the last fifty years. It has not been merely a transformation in size but in orientation as well. The republic was held together by an overarching common vision of a good and just society. It was an incredible political vision, which sought to balance the sometimes conflicting values of freedom and justice with a truly original political system.

However, during the long period of the cold war that vision faded and was replaced by the focus on a common enemy — communism. Being a good American meant being anti-communist. The common enemy provided a very important social glue that held together many diverse groups and hid many internal conflicts. When the great enemy fell (in 1991) it was only a question of time before the search for new enemies would begin. (Grenada, Panama, Sadaam . . . it was only a question of time before the search for enemies turned within — the foreigners, the poor, the war against drugs.) Unless we reclaim some positive vision as a nation, we will be engaged in war upon war upon war. A perpetual state of fear and conflict. Each war creating more enemies. And the vast resources of America will be spent until it loses its economic power, its ability to care for its citizens and to influence the rest of the world.

The fading of a positive common vision coincides with what our artists sense is the beginning of a period of decline. (This is a slow process; it may take a century or two.) It is not observable on the most obvious levels — for America is the richest and most powerful country on earth. But it can be sensed, for those who have eyes to see. The ideal of a better human life has been replaced by the goal of having more. When a common social vision loses its compelling power, liberals turn to protecting their own private worlds of meaning and conservatives seek to impose some form of order on what they see as a fragmented and chaotic situation.

I think that this provides some of the longer and deeper context for understanding the terrible event of 9/11. Those who loved them for many years to come will mourn the dead, but the nation has yet to come to grips with what this event symbolized — the sense that this splendid empire is mortal.

The history of Christianity is helpful in reflecting on this further. Christians had the experience of living in another empire, the Roman Empire. It encompassed the then known world. The empire was repeatedly attacked in its provinces and around the periphery, but in AD 410 the Vandals invaded the city of Rome and burned part of it. Then they left. Rome did not fall on that day. Rome was left standing, and the empire continued on for about another two hundred years. The shock of the sack of Rome reverberated throughout the then known world and provoked Augustine to reflect for the next twelve years on the meaning of this event. Rome did not fall in a day, but in AD 410, for the first time, it seemed not eternal but mortal.

As the decades passed, Christians had to decide how they were going to live in the empire that no longer seemed so eternal. Some continued to work in the empire, contributing to its maintenance and well-being. People raised families and wrote books and lived meaningful lives in their local towns and villages, others cared for those who were being caught in the cataclysm of empire, the military fought off the invasions of the barbarians, some of the senators tried to rescue the senate from the control of the emperor, some preached repentance, and some went out to the edge of empire to build new forms of Christian and social life. In the early monastic communities they took what was best from Rome and combined it with some of the basic values of Christianity in new, practical forms of life.

What was best of Rome survived as the great architecture of the West, the sense of law and politics, and the rights of citizenship. And Rome continued. But it was no longer the center of the world.

We are all called to assess this American Moment — because, at the moment, it has massive implications not only here, but also throughout the world. It is a moment filled with secular visions and ideologies, with religious symbols that are used for many and various purposes.

What does it mean to be patriotic at this moment? What does it mean to be Christian? Do we want to reclaim our republican vision, or do we want to become a great empire? Do we want to be a great nation, or do we want to be a good country? Can we celebrate and trust the ordinary goodness that exists throughout this land? Can we trust this ordinary goodness as much as we fear the enemies? Can we define ourselves by who and what we are for rather than who or what we are against? Which forms of nationhood are worth struggling for as the process of globalization continues?

There are no easy answers here, and it will take great imagination and heart, a sharpness of mind, and a measure of courage to even begin to ask the questions. We must do this for our children.

Within America, the north and the west, there exist immense cultural reservoirs — images and narratives that celebrate the virtues of community, of local citizenship and more modest hopes. There has always been an alternative imagination to the myth of progress and the endless frontier.

I believe that Catholicism has much to offer in this American Moment. To live in America is to live in the center of the world; it is to take here and now as the only point of reference. What Catholicism offers is a tradition, a long tradition that gives importance to the now but not supreme importance. It gives weight to what happens here, but it also takes into account what is happening throughout the universal church. It reminds us that the future of the church (in terms of numbers and vitality) is not here. It is the concerns of others, not ours, that will shape the future of the church. It gives us a different perspective — not one that is always wise but one that we ignore at our own peril. It is this tradition, this catholicity that connects us with the rest of the world in very real ways. Catholicity is much more than some vague sense of the interconnectedness of the universe. It has to do with people, with names and faces and communities to whom we are connected, although they may be quite different from our own.

Ron Rolheiser introduced this symposium urging us to consider our children. More recently, I have found myself taking my lead from them. I know how many of them are deeply concerned about the environment, about the garbage in the world. At times their actions can seem flaky or even fundamentalist, but I do see a new ethic focus emerging from them — a sense that the earth is our common good, what we hold in common. That is a transcendent concern, a concern that flows through and beyond local and national concerns, which is summoning them to new forms of sacrifice and commitment.

I do know that they are summoning us to a depth of Christian life that is as promising for us as it is for them. They do not want or need more words. "We listen to their words but then we see how they live and we know they don't mean what they say." In a time when the texts have worn thin, when the context is sometimes overwhelming, the text of life makes sense. If you want to know what Jesus meant, look at how he lived. If you want to know what the church means, look at how the church lives and acts. There is no shortcut, no easier way.

But this I am beginning to understand. When we take the risk of acting as Jesus acted, living as he lived, we will understand what he meant — and how it is very good news.

Chapter Eight

FROM A PROJECT OF ADAPTATION TO REFOUNDING

Working Out a Guided Image of Mission
in Secularized Societies

Gilles Routhier

A T VARIOUS TIMES during its history, the church has had to answer the question of how to be missionary. Great missionary creativity has been shown in Western society, responding to the challenges of social, economic, and cultural transformations. The twentieth century can be marked by two distinct periods of change: the first half and the second half.

Very simply, the first half of the century can be characterized by the desire to build a Christian city within the framework of emerging industrial society. This period was marked by the rise of social Catholicism, which called for new approaches and resulted in the organization of Catholic trade unions, Catholic cooperatives, the *caisses populaires* (credit unions), the Catholic Farmers Union and the Catholic press, to name a few. During this period, these organizations primarily had the goal of re-Christianizing and transforming society through Catholic works. During the post-war years, these movements experienced a certain "tiredness," and at times their orthodoxy was questioned. Both the cooperative and trade union movements disintegrated. Through transition and renewal, Catholic action was testing itself, and it ultimately failed. This manner of being missionary in this new society did not succeed.

Vatican II seemed to be a moment of synthesis, a time when one acknowledged and "owned" all that preceded it and opened up to new possibilities. These new possibilities were within the new framework of modernity, to which the church tried to reconcile itself after having condemned and fought it for so long. Vatican II marked the beginning of the second period of transformation, which lasted until the 1990s.

During the 1950s, the church had the "feel" of not being able to function anymore. It was operating in circumstances that had radically changed, in which there was no guiding image for the future. In this respect, the 1950s resembled the 1990s. It was apparent that something wasn't working anymore, but the church did not understand what it was yet. It was like a group of children sitting on the edge of a swimming pool, dipping their toes in the water, and daring each other to take the plunge. They test the temperature of the water, but just can't take the risk yet. Without necessarily laying blame, it was undoubtedly a lack of courage or lack of imagination that prevented them from risking new ventures. We recognize that it is not easy to build something when one is old and does not have the resources to do so.

Who is it that builds new houses in our society? Young people do. They are not always rich in resources themselves, but they can build because they have the support of the bank. The church, however, is finding itself older and without those resources, making it more difficult to build those "new houses." At the beginning of the last century, when all the Catholic works were launched, they were rich in resources so it was much easier to imagine the new, and consequently, to be daring. Today, the church finds itself in different circumstances. It could be compared to the situation found in our Canadian health care system. Five billion dollars were cut from the budget at a time when health care was to be completely reconfigured. How do you make something completely new when you are simultaneously deprived of the resources to do it? Despite these circumstances, the Catholic Church does not have to be diverted from its appointment with the Third Millennium.

The proverbial "paradigm shift," an in-depth change of our frame of reference related to the historical situation in which we find ourselves, is necessary for us to switch from a mode of simply adapting to the times to a project of refounding. Refounding entails rediscovering the roles of "founder" and "builder." Adaptation and refounding are two frames of reference that provide ways to reflect, understand, and interpret our present situation. They also will be the frameworks by which we suggest strategies, goals, or objectives to be pursued and designate the means, practices, and persons to achieve those goals.

The first task of adaptation is the project of "leaving behind." As one becomes aware of this step, the *via negativa* presents itself: What do we have to give up and why is it necessary? We must be conscious of where we come from and where we reside at the present moment. It is necessary for us to give up the baggage of our current points of reference and our systems of understanding if we want to graduate from adaptation to a project of refounding.

Those who know Vatican II and its concepts are quite familiar with adaptation. This word appears sixty-three times in the conciliar texts — twelve times in the Constitution on the Liturgy (*Sacrosanctum Concilium*). It makes it possible for the council to assume the project of renewal, to connect the gospel with the street. The theme of adaptation, which in itself involves a whole web of concepts, allows local conditions, the new cultural situation of the West post–World War II, and the rooted diversity of the churches to be taken seriously.

One of the concepts of adaptation involves the correlative term "our time." This expression appears eighty-five times in the conciliar texts. In the Latin texts, *hodie,* or in English "today" occurs ninety-five times. There was nothing like that in the Council of Trent, or in Vatican I. It is significant that Vatican II states "today," referring to the need to adapt. "Our time" occurs eighty-five times in the Constitution on the Sacred Liturgy alone. For example, it says that during Lent, penance should not only be internal and individual, but external and social. The practice of penance "should be fostered in ways that are possible in our own times and in different regions and according to the circumstances of the faithful" (*SC* V, 110).

This quotation helps us move from a temporal consideration (our time, today) to a spatial consideration of diverse regions. It allows local customs and traditions of various regions to be considered. For instance, in the funeral rites, it is possible to adapt the liturgical language to the particular customs of a region. There is a similar consideration regarding the celebration of marriage: "If any regions are wont to use other praiseworthy customs and ceremonies when celebrating the sacrament of matrimony, the sacred synod earnestly desires that these by all means be retained" (*SC* III, 77). The location of the church, both temporally ("our time") and spatially, thus holds an important place in conciliar reflection with regard to the Constitution on the Liturgy.

The need for adaptation opened up the need for a new understanding of the diversity of the roots of the church, which "has no wish to impose a rigid uniformity in matters which do not implicate the faith or the good of the whole community; rather does she respect and foster the genius and talents of various races and peoples" (*SC* III, D, 37).

During Vatican II, at least in its official language, the Catholic Church began a revision of its understanding of universality, which corresponded to its awakening to two major historical phenomena: the decolonization of the South and the cultural change encompassing the West. Decolonization made it possible to surpass Eurocentrism, which had characterized missions up to that point. The church did not consider the full extent of the second phenomenon, the cultural shift of the West; however, it did sense that shift was distant from its own fundamental premises. Its pastoral action during Vatican II tried to adjust to the circumstances of time and place, and these adjustments seemed to touch on all dimensions of its life, but the church still could not imagine the extent and depth of the change that was required.

Adaptation is limited when applied only to external forms, but certain conciliar indications point to an opening for changes of a much greater depth. Consider this excerpt from *Ad Gentes*, which says that mission should relate to all the spheres of activity in the church: "Finally the faith is taught by an adequate catechesis; it is celebrated in a liturgy in harmony with the genius of the people, and by suitable canonical legislation, it is introduced into upright institutions and local customs" (*AG* 19). This quotation tells us that in the life of the church, first, we must adapt the manner of announcing the gospel; second, we must celebrate that in a "liturgy in harmony with the genius of the people"; and third, in the ecclesial government of the church, canonical legislation is to be introduced to support institutions and local customs. In short, these areas of the church have to be adapted. Vatican II will never be able to free itself from the problems of adaptation of which it remains a prisoner, and the importance of the references in the Constitution on the Liturgy cannot be overlooked.

Vatican II worked with another concept of equal importance, that of *instauratio*, or restoration. There are sixteen references to it in the document on the liturgy. The term is also found in the preamble and acts as an organizing concept for the first chapter, entitled "General Principles for the Restoration and Promotion of the Sacred Liturgy"; paragraphs 21 and 40 of Chapter III use the word "restoration" six

times. We also find the concept of restoration in other conciliar documents, in particular, *Ad Gentes,* which proposes the
restoration of the diaconate, and *Christus Dominus,* which
proposes the restoration of the catechumenate. This prospect
for progress via restoration enters into the conciliar corpus
largely by means of the liturgical movement.

The new forms leave the existing forms in place to some
extent. According to the tradition of the church, becoming modern means adapting and restoring old forms. The
examination of the linguistic style that characterizes the Constitution on the Liturgy is revealing in the manner that it
includes and understands these things. The council perceived
that the church was in a new situation both in the Western
and non-Western worlds, but it did not think it was necessary to re-invent it, or create something new. They felt that it
was simply a question of adapting to a new time and space,
an adjustment of the existing Christian institutions to the
new situation. *Aggiornamiento* (renewal) was understood in
terms of *instauration* (restoration). This approach to thinking in Christianity runs throughout the twentieth century. It
comes from the belief that if present ways were adapted and
restored, the problems would vanish. There is disillusionment
with this type of conciliar thinking. It isn't the council itself
that caused the disenchantment but the belief that while the
restoration and adaptation were happening, things were going
to return to how they had been before.

While some say that the church should take old approaches
and adapt them, there are others who say that because the
church is operating in a new context, a different approach is
needed. It is like trying to sew a patch of fabric on old clothing;
it is not surprising that it still tears. Or you put an addition on
a house rather than daring to build a new one. We must "refound" the Christian experience, moving from restructuration
to invention. We are entering into a new stage in the history
of Christianity in the West; we live in a new world, one in

which the church cannot simply dream of reestablishment, reconquest, or restoration.

Today the strategies of adaptation in the church seem to be exhausted, and many are unhappy with the attempts to restructure. Rather than adapting to the modern world, we are more concerned with adapting church resources, for example, the fewer number of priests. If you look in all the dioceses where pastoral restructuring has been done, the mission of the church is quite present in the rhetoric; however, the restructuring remains lacking of any creativity capable of refounding the church in the current context. This restructuring process is at a major disadvantage if the overall presence of the church in society is not considered and the focus is on the "retirement" of the church because of shrinking parish ministry. By simply reducing the priestly services of the parish, the last defended area, we are thinking we are safeguarding at least something of Christendom.

It has been said that "parish is a missionary community." By making the parish a community, and then by saying that the parish will be missionary from now on, indicates that the parish is meant to be the missionary agent of the church. The idea is that by turning everything over to the parishes, they will become missionary communities. It is also said that a church that is moving, enticing, and involving determines the perception of those who either usually attend it or go by chance. If a community is on fire, cordial, and appealing, mission would evolve from that.

It is also said that through the liturgy "there is a world that awaits us." Since many people pass through a parish, and it is through the parish that they have contact with the priest, the parish must have a role to play in the evangelization of people. The liturgy is the central pastoral and sacramental "project" of the church. It is people who are already practicing their faith, who are already Christian, who come to the parish, giving us the possibility of parochial influence. We assume then that people will benefit from even initial contact with the parish, and that instruction will give birth to Christians. Those ideas, born in the 1940s, continue to this day: that a project of evangelization, which can be started in the parish with the ministering of sacraments, can be accomplished while trying to build living communities.

It should not be assumed, however, that the parish could be the means for the mission. We need to realize that in fact the parochial network was not conceived for mission but for the pastoral structuring of the faithful. It was designed for the care of the baptized and for a stable pastoral center or gathering place. In its present form, it is perfectly adapted to a time in Christendom when secular space and religious space correspond or when the parochial connects the church and the social field. In its current form, the parochial network shows serious limits in spite of adjustments, renewal, and adaptation of parishes.

Pastoral practice, as well, corresponds to a state of Christianity that rests on the activity of the clergy. Today, when one lacks clergy, one makes new clergy and religious. This practice does not prioritize the state of the baptized without playing into the opposition between evangelization and sacramentalization. It does not lay a foundation, starting from the breaking open of the word, nor from sacramentalization as participation in worship. Parochial action, its privileged ground, is the gathered community. It is space connected with the church, distinguished as good, as opposed to the situation of dissemination and dispersion in common secular space. The principal actors in parishes are the ordained ministers, who render pastoral services to those who require and claim them. However, in a highly secularized society of post-Christianity, we need a pastoral practice that values the mission without neglecting the pastoral care of the faithful.

We need another practice or device, separate from the parish, that values mission. We need a pastoral action sufficiently mobile enough to venture onto the terrain of the "other," one that does not just remain on parochial ground in a society where all do not adhere explicitly to Christ. We need to remember that not all people want to develop their membership with the church. Without minimizing the essential contribution of ordained ministers, religious congregations, or any other pastoral persons in charge, it should be recognized that in such a society, the gospel of God will be passed through laypeople who live in the secular world to those who do not believe. Dispersion, or dissemination, can take priority over gathering in a parochial structure. It is necessary to recognize that our current institutional network is not adapted to pastoral productivity or accompaniment. The starting point of a missionary pastorate is church membership that is not given by birth, custom, or sociological pressure, but one that is acquired by choice and decision.

While the goal that leads the effort of pastoral restructuring is the mission, we will not be able to renew that mission if we simply reorganize parishes and change their borders. Rather than just looking at parochial networks, the pastoral practices of whole dioceses need to be reexamined in a complete and imaginative way. If we are not willing to do so, restructuring and adapting the parish will always give disappointing and insufficient results in reaching the goals of missionary activity. Missionary activity is the principal activity of the church. This was especially true when the church was not yet rooted in a place or when the preaching of the word was not yet intended to cause the first gathering. There is confusion when "parish" and "mission of the parish" are thought to be two correlative terms. The parish evokes stability, roots, the established church, and a sedentary nature. It was brought into being after the church had a few years of missionary activity and then constituted itself into a place.

Whereas the parish is church gathered around the word and a place for the pastoral care of Christians, mission represents the activity of the church working in the medium of a world that has not yet heard the word. Fundamentally, the mission is an itinerant activity, and as such it is necessary to find a pastoral method that makes us itinerant rather than sedentary. It must be a pastoral method that implies "sending" and going out toward the broad world, to a space where the gospel has not yet been announced or heard. Missionary action requires forms of activities distinct from the parish. Even if a parish can develop some activities proper to mission, by design it was set up for initiation into Christian life for those who want to become Christian and for the pastoral care of the faithful. It is necessary for parishes to continue to exist for those reasons, but to do so within a more complex pastoral system. We must have something else to ensure the service of mission institutionally. Passing from a Christian world to a primarily missionary situation, from a religious world to a highly secularized society, demands not only an overall re-examination of the parochial network but a radical look at all of the activity of the church up to the present time. Pastoral restructuring cannot be reduced to repairing or adapting what remains, nor should it be limited to the parochial domain. The pastoral situation we find ourselves in encourages the use of creativity and imagination to restructure our whole pastoral system and undertake total reform, something beyond a simple facelift or a replastering of a façade. It is a time for building.

We are faced with a double challenge of acknowledging the circumstances of modernity and of becoming a church in a state of mission. This double challenge asserts itself at a moment when there is a shortage of priests and a general reduction in the resources the church has had up until now. Neither of these circumstances simplifies this task. The greatest risks the church appears to be facing are the retreat into reduced parochial ministry and the avoidance of not facing this challenge of mission. These risks would play out in taking refuge, if not in the parish, then in the four great functions that give the church its current social respectability at a time when the welfare state is disengaged.

First of all, society is ready to accept the church provided that it transforms itself into a giant St. Vincent de Paul Society that doesn't speak about God, Christ, or the paschal mystery. Second, society is ready to continue to tolerate or accept the church if it is willing to be the servant of public religion, offering rites of passage to children and national marriages and funerals of movie stars. The church becomes a supplier of civic religion for symbolic Christians. The third way that society accepts the church is if it limits itself to speaking about values and ethics, provided it does not speak about Christian spirituality. The fourth way is as a vehicle to recycle our cultural heritage and all that goes along with it. Taking greater refuge in our parishes, in its affairs, perpetuates the thinking that "all is well, the world accepts us." People come to the church when they need a baptism, we organize soup kitchens and clothing giveaways, and everything is beautiful.

Rather than consider the future of the church, I prefer to propose another vision of the place and role of the church in society. The church is, first, at the service of the gospel and the reign of God. This is where we must devote the bulk of our efforts and resources. With this in mind, I will propose and develop three complementary paths.

The first task is to diffuse the gospel by capillary vessels. In our body, there are not simply arteries and veins but a whole capillary network running blood and oxygen to all its parts. If we do not want the gospel to become either marginalized or reduced to a tiny space of worship, but diffused in the whole of society as leaven, it is necessary that it be widely diffused by a capillary network. This means that the gospel first must be carried into various modes of life by the baptized to act there as leaven for restoration. If we do not take on this priority task, we are complicit in the marginalization of Christianity.

Vatican II identified some particular arenas for this diffusion of the gospel to happen: science and culture; family life; economic, political, and social activity; promotion of solidarity among people and nations; safeguarding peace. This is the

plan of the second part of *Gaudium et Spes*. Today we can perhaps add other areas: promotion of human dignity; defense of
human rights; safeguarding creation; advancements in knowledge and technology. The Catholic Church is equipped at
both the national and international levels with institutions
that ensure the presence of the gospel in these various areas.
Rome and other episcopal conferences are already present in
important forums where these affairs are discussed. The prob
lem is that in these domains, laypeople are absent and that
connection to the gospel in the social realm is missing.

Take, for example, the issue of bioethics. We do not need
new episcopal messages or encyclicals on bioethics. What is
needed are Christian doctors on bioethics committees in hospitals who carry the gospel message. That will have the most
determining influence on day-to-day decisions. It is the same
in the field of social ethics. It is important to have Christian
people on councils that manage pension funds rather than a
new social encyclical on the subject. These connections do not
exist in the present social realm because laypeople have not
been formed for missionary work in this time and situation.
My first priority for building would be to accompany and train
Christian men and women in being the capillary network that
carries the gospel through society. After showing their engagement and enthusiasm, Christians will then again take to heart
the appeal of John XXIII, who began all his encyclicals with
the statement "With all people of goodwill ... "

Laity who assume the role of a significant Christian presence in our society have nearly disappeared. In various
dimensions of their social life, their vision of the world, and
their adopted strategies of commitment, they are forced to
remain silent about the Christian inspiration of their actions. There was a generation of Christians, formed mainly
through the Catholic action groups to which I referred earlier,
that worked in the 1960s and 1970s in various political par-
ties, trade unions, and multiple special-interest groups. They

began eagerly and with hope, expecting the advent of a better and more human world. The next generation, after the 1980s, emerged to find a devastated field of Catholic laity. In spite of that, Christians still represent an important group, not only in the area of charitable action but also in significant social movements: women's issues, the fight against poverty, defending the rights of immigrants, to name a few. Today, confronted more and more with Western society's vision of religion as a strictly private affair and a system of ethics largely inspired by utilitarianism, Christians have to regroup and instead must develop relevant social practices. We cannot continue to count on the heritage left by the Catholic action movements of history and develop a model of presence that corresponds to our time and culture.

Our task is to develop a model of support for North American Christian laity. That model must start from their own religious convictions and convey the gospel in situations common to both Christians and non-Christians. Is it possible for believers to transform the world, starting from a dialogue inspired by religious conviction within the framework of common practices in society? Today Christians find themselves isolated from each other, silent, without the possibility of debate and reflection on models of society or social structures. Does it not fall to them, more than anyone else, to support the quality of interpersonal relationships around them? Take the example of Christian nurses. Their only manner of living the gospel, since health care is secularized so much, will be to support good interpersonal relationships with those around them. They may take refuge in practicing charity at church or in other philanthropic works that compensate for the worst effects of our society, but they are without the benefit of developing solid analysis of systems of which they are a part. We must develop and support opportunities that would make it possible for Christians to gather, giving them means of acting in the name of their faith as agents of transformation and giving them opportunities for prayer, witness, and good works. A common example of this is prayer lunches among professionals. I know of meetings of Christians who are in parliament, Christian business associations, and more recently, an international forum on management, ethics, and spirituality. The first undertaking for building is gathering, forming, and accompanying Christians who journey to all levels of society.

The second area of building is the circulation of the gospel into the arteries of social life. If we do not do this, the church will be increasingly marginalized over time. Besides the capillary network of the baptized and apart from the parish reality, we must establish a presence in the most secular areas. We must think of a more institutional presence in the areas of health care and education in different ways than in the past. The same goes for the areas of social and international solidarity, culture, communications, and economics. We need to be acting through decision makers, researchers, families, young people. The church may reserve a place in society for the celebration of sacraments, but it will not be allowed to share its particular perspective of the world in the name of the gospel, anticipating the coming of God's kingdom. We must not agree to the privatization of religion and must ensure that the gospel is present in public space. If the gospel is to remain in the public forum, society, as Paul VI said, and not simply individuals, must be evangelized. The gospel must be able to be found in the widest possible social networks and institutions.

The church must be made present in those social networks through people exclusively dedicated to this purpose who have the mission of returning the gospel and church to these arteries of society. We must be comfortable in these networks and be present in all aspects of them; if we do not, the gospel will be confined to our cloisters. While our presence seems to be assured at the national level, it is the interecclesial and interreligious coalitions that, starting from a critical analysis of the evolution of society, speak of and propose independent action. During the last few years, they have led campaigns to fight poverty, forgive the debt of developing nations, dispute models of universalization that reduce globalization to market economy, support environmental protection, and urge reflection on cloning and genetic engineering. There is still much work to do, and perhaps it is the role of the Catholic universities, or any other centers of Catholic thought, to do it. These practices dispute the current model of society; they articulate vigorous criticism of the market economy's absolute power and techno-science's contempt for any humanistic vision. It is necessary to be involved in these matters at all levels — national, regional, and local.

The third area for building is ensuring the presence of the church through a flexible institutional network, which I call "district houses." While the first two points brought forward levels of Christian presence indispensable for the entire evangelical activity, this third level of presence must be found in the dwelling places of the men, women, and children of today. The church must be obvious and easily locatable in the weave of neighborhoods and cities; it must have a place on the street and be easily visible. Given such a presence, would parishes be necessary? I would say no, but there may be different opinions on this subject. I believe that all is not accomplished on the parochial level. Parishes cannot do everything, and I imagine that soon some parishes will not be able to fulfill the range of requirements, not for lack of resources, finances, or priests but for lack of the faithful. There still should be a tangible presence of the church, supported by Christians in a particular location in each neighborhood or area of a city. This is what I call a "district house"; multifunctional in nature, it is often a house of charity and culture, and serves as a gathering place.

In the West, the church must take up a challenge that was unknown in the past. It needs to offer places not merely for the structuring of the faithful or for Christian initiation, but spaces for the first contact or proclamation of the gospel, an initial experiment with Christian life. A multifunctional house will facilitate the institutional passage from a pastorate of structures, based on the parochial boundaries of a diocesan territory, to a pastorate of productivity that is sensitive to the searching and the questions of our contemporaries. It will be for those who are distanced from parishes, who fear them like the plague, because they fear being caught and brought back, but still need some connection. Those who are distanced and fear turning up at a parish are afraid to be caught up in an invitation of embarking into community.

I worked a little in the education of adults, in which there is a "law" that "the least educated fear school like the plague." This is because they do not feel culturally comfortable in school. They feel ill at ease because they are afraid to be ridiculed if they cannot read. The jump is too high. In these cases, education can take place in less institutionalized spaces. The elimination of illiteracy is accomplished on kitchen tables and not in classrooms. For the non-Christian, entering a parish is too high of a jump; re-education is more likely to take place in particularly hospitable settings.

These district houses and houses of charity can be multifunctional in nature. Houses of charity are places of learning to live in solidarity, of being close to those in need, of learning to share, and of helping one another move from formation to involvement in the spirit of the gospel. For example, they are places where one can establish projects like a communal kitchen or a society of mutual aid; they are where resources can be found and networks can be formed. District houses can become a space where human beings find, exchange, and share reasons to hope, as well as share a meal. They will undoubtedly be places where God, who as Jesus the Servant, could once again say his name: "God saves."

These culture houses would be a way to support those who are coming into first contact with the Christian tradition by offering a space to meet and converse with believers. Workshops combined with activities, for both adults and children, can do this. Workshops on stained glass or icons, conferences, discussion circles or philosophical debates, drama, and book-shops are a few examples of what can be done. It is through culture and the arts that people can be reached and questions of faith can be raised. It is undoubtedly by this approach that many of our contemporaries, eager to know more about Christ, first approached the Christian tradition and tamed the gospel — by coming to know more about the community connected with the church.

These culture houses would make it possible to live the first stage in the spreading of the gospel. They would offer people the occasion to let the words of Christ resound in their hearts: "Come and see." These multifunctional houses should be places of knowledge, places where you are reminded not only to enter into and practice silence, but also to appropriate the word of God, listen to it, and share it. There would be possibilities for spiritual accompaniment in the journey of faith and discernment of the will of God in order to follow Christ, to live in his spirit and better serve our brothers and sisters. There could be opportunities to celebrate the sacrament of reconciliation, or at least be listened to.

There are other areas to be mentioned. It is necessary to be present in public communications. If we are not, we are socially nonexistent. It is also necessary to develop intermediate structures of network centers, large sanctuaries of education, a mobile pastorate, and, after that, parishes and cathedrals. It is possible to invent, re-create, and rediscover the movements and motions of builders.

It is urgent to pass from the logic of adaptation to the logic of creation.

Chapter Nine

EVANGELIZING
THE AMERICAN CULTURE

Robert Barron

I N THIS PRESENTATION I should like to reflect on the challenge of evangelizing in the properly American context, but I would like to state at the outset what must characterize any and all attempts to announce the good news. To evangelize is to proclaim Jesus Christ crucified and risen from the dead. When this kerygma, this paschal mystery, is not at the heart of the project, Christian evangelization effectively disappears, devolving into a summons to bland religiosity or generic spirituality. When Jesus crucified and risen is not proclaimed, a beige and unthreatening Catholicism emerges, a thought system that is, at best, an echo of the environing culture. Peter Maurin, one of the founders of the Catholic Worker movement, said that the church has taken its own dynamite, placed it in hermetically sealed containers, and sat on the lid. In a similar vein, Stanley Hauerwas commented that the problem with Christianity is not that it is socially conservative or politically liberal, but that "it is just too damned dull"! For both Maurin and Hauerwas, what leads to this attenuation is a refusal to preach the dangerous and unnerving news concerning Jesus risen from the dead.

But how do we accomplish this uncompromising evangelistic task in an American culture marked by pluralism, secularism, and religious diversity? How do we manage to say, in a way that is not arrogant, violent, or divisive, that Jesus Christ crucified and risen is of central importance? How do we make persuasive this surprising and counter-intuitive claim? I will try to answer these questions, first, by examining in some detail what is at stake in the central Christian affirmation; second, by assessing the American cultural situation in terms of its openness and resistance to the gospel message; and, third, by suggesting some concrete practices for effective evangelization.

The *Communio* Vision

When a Christian speaks the good news about Jesus' resurrection, she is not simply talking about an extraordinary turn of events in the life of a particular individual. Rather, she is making a claim about the deepest structure of reality, about the way things, at their most basic level, are. According to the biblical witness, Jesus is not simply a great man, a prophet, a seer, or a social reformer; he is the Word of God made flesh, which is to say, the intelligibility of being made present in visible, iconic form. A first consequence of this incarnational sensibility is that the death of Jesus must be construed as judgment on the world, *the* sign that all is not well with us. As Peter says in his kerygmatic discourse in Acts, "the Lord of life came and you put him to death." There must be something fundamentally askew in those who sought to eliminate, in the most brutally violent way, the bearer of the divine presence. It is important to note too, following Hans Urs von Balthasar, that the New Testament symbolically includes everyone in this judgment by showing how disciples, Romans, and Jews all contributed to his death.

If Jesus had simply remained in his grave, he would have been one of a thousand inspiring and failed religious figures who have emerged in the course of time, one more prophet, in Albert Schweitzer's words, "ground under by the wheel of history." But the evangelical claim is that he appeared alive

to his disciples after his death, still bearing the marks of cru-
cifixion and uttering a message of peace. Both of those details
are significant. In most of the resurrection narratives, Jesus
makes explicit reference to his wounds, inviting his disciples
to see or, in the case of Thomas, to touch them. It is said that
Teresa of Avila was able to see through a ruse of the devil ap-
pearing to her in the guise of the risen Christ. "Be gone," she
said, "you have no wounds." The marks on the body of Jesus
are signs of the violence that killed him and hence symbols of
a perverted love of violence radically at odds with God's way
of being. Seeing our own dysfunction in them is an essential
aspect of the paschal experience.

But having shown his wounds, Jesus does something utterly
surprising: he speaks a word of peace. In Luke's account of
the appearance to the eleven, the disciples are terrified when
the risen Christ comes upon them. This is not only because
they are seeing something novel and unexpected; it is also because they sense that the murdered man, in accord with the
structure of the classic ghost story, is back, undoubtedly to
seek vengeance on those who denied, betrayed, and abandoned
him. From ancient myths to contemporary crime stories, the
rhythm remains the same: order destroyed through violence
is restored through an answering violence. But the crucified
and risen Christ — the most unjustly persecuted victim in
history — does not respond with violence; instead, he says,
"Shalom." The disorder of the cross, the killing of the Son of
God, is restored, but through compassion and forgiving love.
This is the novelty and revelation contained in the paschal
mystery: the true God is not a practitioner or sanctioner of
sacred violence; he is the one whose being and action have
nothing to do with violence and vengeance. St. John would
put it this way: "God is light; in him there is no darkness."
Humanity killed the Lord of life, and God returned in compassion, which is why St. Paul could exclaim, "I am certain that
neither death nor life, neither angels nor principalities, neither
height nor depth, nor any other creature could ever separate

us from the love of God that comes to us in Christ Jesus our Lord." Psychologists have said that a friend is someone who has seen you at your worst and still loves you. Thus, when the old spiritual says, "what a friend we have in Jesus," it is not trading in pious rhetoric; rather it is getting to the heart of the matter. The death and resurrection of Jesus proves that God is our friend, because God has seen us at our worst and still loves us.

If God has disclosed himself as friendship and compassionate love, he must *be* friendship and compassionate love in his own most reality, and this entails that in God there must be a play of lover, beloved, and shared love. Accordingly, the idea that God is himself a *communio* of persons, a Trinity of Father, Son, and Spirit, flows from the surprise of the paschal mystery. It is, of course, in the Gospel of John that the connection between the drama of salvation and the trinitarian nature of God is first made unmistakably clear. The prologue to John articulates the distinctiveness of the divine being as co-inherence and co-implication: "In the beginning was the Word and the Word was with God and the Word was God." The true God is not a monolith, not a supreme substance, but a family, a conversation, a play of speaker, spoken and speech. By insisting, furthermore, that the Word *is* God, John implies that the divine persons are not together as "ball bearings in a bucket" but rather as interacting and overlapping fields of force.

As the prologue unfolds, we see the implications of this understanding of God for a theology of creation: "All things came into being through him, and without him not one thing came into being" (John 1:3). So accustomed are we to the language and cadence of this verse that we might overlook its radicality. In both mythological and philosophical accounts of creation prior to Christianity, the being and order of the world emerge through a primal violence or manipulation. In the mythic framework, creation occurs through the battle of the gods and in the philosophical matrix, as in Plato and Aristotle, for example, cosmic order is established through the formation of matter. We glimpse in John something radically different, what theologians will later formulate as a doctrine of *creatio ex nihilo*, creation from nothing. When the true God creates, he doesn't manipulate, dominate, or wrestle into submission anything outside of himself, but rather through a sheerly generous and nonviolent act of love, he gives rise to the totality of finite reality. And because this act is *ex nihilo*, there is literally nothing that stands between God's causal presence and that which he makes. Therefore, even as he remains ontologically distinct from the world, God is, to paraphrase Augustine, closer to creation than creation is to itself. In short, the *communio* universe nests nonviolently in the primordial *communio* of the Trinity.

A further implication of the doctrine of creation from nothing is that all of God's creatures are intimately connected to one another in an echo of the primordial co-inherence of the Trinitarian persons. Since all creation is centered in God, all finite things, despite their enormous differences in size, position, quality, or metaphysical status, are linked together as ontological siblings. When Francis of Assisi spoke of "brother sun and sister moon," he was using language not only poetically evocative but also metaphysically precise. All creatures are like islands in an archipelago, separate on the surface, but connected at the depths.

In the blazing light of the paschal mystery — Jesus crucified and risen from the dead — the first Christians saw the very structure of the divine being and the deepest truth about the world that God has made. In Jesus, the icon of the invisible God, they understood that Existence is co-inherence, compassion, nonviolent being-for-the-other. To proclaim this vision — with its political, social, economic, artistic, cultural, and indeed cosmic implications — is what evangelization means in the broadest sense.

I would like to close this section by attending to just a few expressions of the *communio* vision that have emerged in the course of the Catholic tradition. One of the most striking features of the Gothic cathedrals is the rose window. The rose is a wheel of light and color, all of whose elements are focused around a center that is invariably a depiction of Christ. Accordingly, it is a symbol of the well ordered psyche, the well-ordered city, the well-ordered cosmos. When all of the energies of one's soul — intellect, will, emotions, creativity, sexuality — are given over to Christ and grounded in him, then they exist in and for one another in a sort of psychological co-inherence. When all of the activities of a city — administration, economic production, artistic enterprise, and recreation — are oriented to Christ, then they too co-inhere creatively in one another. The demons in the Gospels — speaking so often in the plural — symbolize the loss of psychological and spiritual *communio*: "What do you want with us, Jesus of Nazareth?" This is the voice of the disintegrated self, the splintered community, each element at war with the others. Jesus preaches this *communio* message when he says, "Seek ye first the kingdom of God and his righteousness, and the rest will be given unto you." In other words, find the center, and the periphery will tend to fall into place around it.

We find something similar in Dante's vision at the end of the *Divine Comedy*. Gazing toward the heart of the heavenly host, Dante sees the saints and angels clustered around the light of God and forming a harmonic display, much like a white rose. In his autobiography *Seven Storey Mountain*, Thomas Merton remembers the little French town of St.-Antonin, where he spent some of his childhood. The village was arranged in such a way that all of the streets led, like spokes, to the cathedral, so that wherever one walked, one was drawn, ineluctably, toward the spiritual center. Later in the *Seven Storey Mountain*, Merton saw the Abbey of Gethsemani in a similar light, describing it as the axis of the country, the secret center around which everything else turned. The

most philosophically precise account of the *communio* view
is Thomas Aquinas's theology of participation. For Aquinas,
all finite things, from archangels to stones, participate in the
to-be of God, who is the sheer act of existence. This in turn
entails that all created things are interrelated, constituting an
artistic work in progress, contributing to an overall design and
purpose. All of these expressions — artistic, poetic, metaphysical — flow from and in their own manner articulate the good
news of Jesus Christ crucified and risen from the dead.

The Compromising of the *Communio* Vision: Protestantism and Secularism

Having spelled out in some detail the nature of the Catholic *communio* vision, I would like to examine the process
by which that vision was, in both Protestantism and modern secularism, to varying degrees compromised, questioned,
undermined. This examination is pertinent to our subject
precisely in the measure that American culture has been so
thoroughly shaped by these two great forces.

So many of the great Reformers were trained in the philosophical school of nominalism, with its roots in the speculations of the late medieval Franciscan William of Occam.
Like his Franciscan predecessor Duns Scotus, Occam held to
a univocal conception of being, according to which both the
infinite existence of God and the finite existence of creatures
are instances of a general, overarching category of being that
contains them both. In sharp contrast to Aquinas's analogi-
cal understanding of being, this view effectively situates God
and creatures side by side as discrete existents against a common ontological background. Though God is infinite and the
creature finite, both are beings without an essential connection to one another. Thus the participation of creatures in
God is denied and, as a consequence, the interconnection between creatures is attenuated. Indeed William of Occam can
say *praeter illas partes absolutas nulla res est* (outside of these

absolute parts, there is nothing), signaling the triumph of the disassociated individual.

It is not difficult to discern certain nominalist themes in the writings and preaching of the Reformers. Martin Luther throughout his career was a great defender of the divine transcendence and hence remained suspicious of all appeals to mysticism and sacramentalism, anything that would collapse the radical distinction between God and the world or suggest that God was available in creation. This denial of participation metaphysics conduced, as in Scotus and Occam, to a stress on the isolated individual — which can be seen in the theologies of both Luther and John Calvin. In Luther's case, the spiritual drama centers around the justification of the individual discernible in the very private act of faith; and in Calvin's case, the focus is on the predestination of the individual, readable through certain signs both interior and exterior. For both Reformers, the *communio* of the church, the co-inherent circle of believers, and the *communio* of creation, the co-inherent circle of things made *ex nihilo*, become secondary at best. Though essential elements of the Christian proclamation obviously remain in the Reformers, we do witness in their theology an attenuating of the *communio*/participation vision that held sway through the High Middle Ages.

This compromising of *communio* becomes, however, more dramatically apparent in the secular version of Protestantism that is philosophical modernity. The non-sacramental world of the Reformers becomes the disenchanted universe *tout court* in most of the moderns. Particularly instructive here is the thought of Thomas Hobbes. A thorough materialist, Hobbes held that reality is nothing but particles in motion, and his most famous application of this metaphysic was in the arena of politics and social theory. In the state of nature, human beings are isolated monads, motivated by the dominant passions to survive and to avoid violent death. The inevitable conflict of antagonistic egos (particles bouncing painfully off one another) produces a life that is, in Hobbes's famous phrase, "solitary, poor, nasty, brutish and short," and this state of affairs, in turn, gives rise to the desire to enter into a social contract. Mind you, the forming of civil society has nothing to do with a classical conception of justice or the good life, and it is by no means the consequence of our essentially social nature, just the contrary. It is the attempt by a collectivity of self-interested individuals to mitigate the threat to life and limb that each presents to the other. The Hobbesian government (the Leviathan) is instituted precisely for the purpose of protection and not direction, any sense of social teleology precluded by Hobbes's metaphysics. A generation after Hobbes, John Locke produced a somewhat kinder and gentler version of this account. Though he retained strands of the medieval synthesis — the existence of a distant, rather Deist God and a truncated form of the natural law — Locke still saw government's purpose as protective of individual rights to life, liberty, and property.

Another extremely influential element in the modern secular conception of government was the insistence on the privatization of religion. In the wake of the wars between Catholics and Protestants that plagued Europe in the century or so after the Reformation, most modern thinkers — Locke, Spinoza, Leibniz, Kant, and Hegel are examples — opted for a rational version of religion that could, on account of its reasonability, aspire to universality. Concomitantly, they encouraged a privatization of positive or revealed religion: such expressions — and their attendant practices — could be tolerated as long as they did not extrude into the public realm of politics, economics, and social relations. Stanley Hauerwas has referred to this arrangement as "the modern peace treaty" with religion and has noticed how neatly it fit with the subjectivized versions of Christianity encouraged within Protestantism. The sequestration of faith within the confines of subjectivity, combined with the acceptance of a fundamentally antagonistic social ontology, spelled the dissolution of the *communio* vision during the early modern period.

Protestantism, Modernity, and American Culture

It is obviously a daunting task to name the elements that go into the shaping of a culture as rich and complex as America's. However, I think that it is not too wide of the mark to say that the two movements we have been describing, namely, Protestantism and secular modernity, have played an especially powerful role in influencing American culture in both style and substance. Cardinal Francis George of Chicago expressed this dual influence with both humor and precision, saying that America was formed largely by "Calvin and Hobbes."

Let us look first at "Calvin." We have seen that the great Reformers stressed the inner experience of the individual believer, as the Holy Spirit, in either justification or predestination, made himself known. When Protestant theology became more rationalized through the speculations of seventeenth-century theologians, groups such as the Moravians, the Hutterites, the Anabaptists, the Quakers, and the Puritans re-emphasized the role of inner experience or inner light. It is of no small importance that these groups were particularly well represented in the settling of the American colonies. Thus an already subjectivized Protestantism took on an even more radically interior and experiential form in this country. We can see it in the Wesleyan and holiness traditions of tracking one's inner experience of God and giving expression to it in vivid and bodily ways, or of the Quaker insistence that no one speaks in church until convicted by the Spirit. Also, from the colonial period through the middle of the nineteenth century, American Protestantism was fired regularly by revivals and tent meetings, forums where the keen sense of having been born again or converted were paramount. In more recent times, this tradition has been continued by evangelists from Billy Sunday to Billy Graham.

A more rarified and intellectual form of this subjectivism can be discerned in the liberal Protestantism flowing from

Friedrich Schleiermacher and his disciples. Raised in a Moravian community, Schleiermacher never lost his keen awareness of the inner light, even as he transposed it into the feeling of absolute dependency. Schleiermacher's influence in our culture, mediated through the universities and the more sophisticated pulpits, can be seen in Yankee Unitarianism and eventually in Emerson's transcendentalism and Walt Whitman's pantheist mysticism. And these movements, in their turn, helped to feed, in more recent years, many forms of New Age spirituality, a movement that clearly emphasizes the inner states of the individual. I can't help but see, too, a purely secular expression of this tradition in the American cult of the talk show, that forum in which one is encouraged (even compelled) to manifest his inner states and experiences to an audience both fascinated and repelled.

Now lest this discussion become simplistic and unbalanced, it is most important to note certain features of American Protestantism that cannot be easily correlated to subjectivism and individualism. There has indeed been, perhaps despite itself, a politically and socially conscious form of Protestant religiosity in America. It can be seen in the Emancipation movement that shook the country profoundly in the middle of the nineteenth century; in the Social Gospel of Rauschenbusch and others at the beginning of the twentieth century; in the civil rights movement of the 1950s and 1960s that came surging up out of black churches vividly aware of the implications for liberation in the biblical revelation; and in the radical nonviolence of the Mennonite tradition expressed by John Howard Yoder and Stanley Hauerwas in very recent years. These I would read as remnants of the *communio* vision, still available despite the individualist revolution wrought by the Reformers. As we shall see later, the canny Catholic evangelist should be especially sensitive to these vestiges.

Now let us turn to "Hobbes." The fundamentally antagonistic social ontology of Hobbes, and its attendant agnosti-
cism about ultimate ends, can be clearly seen in the founding
political documents of our nation. According to Thomas
Jefferson's Declaration of Independence, the purpose of government is the protection of one's threatened rights to life,
liberty and the pursuit of happiness. The last of this famous
trio is perhaps the most interesting. Though the individual
citizen's right to *seek* happiness is guaranteed, no indication
whatsoever is given as to the telos of that quest. In accordance
with the modern peace treaty, the determination of that goal
remains a purely private matter, not subject to public adju-
dication. Thus, the society outlined by Jefferson and given
formal structure in the Constitution is one that is protective
and not directive. As Robert Kraynak has argued, this modern
understanding of the self and its relation to government has
conduced to a certain societal vapidity and loss of purpose:
the Jeffersonian subject is well protected, but he has no idea
where to go. Many commentators have seen the effects of this
social philosophy in the shocking violence, litigiousness, and
moral drift in our society. All of this obviously makes difficult
the task of Christian evangelization, since the *communio* vision is at odds, not only with an antagonistic individualism,
but also with a social space void of teleology. The dying and
rising of Jesus *have* to affect politics, economics, social theory, business, entertainment — all of the public dimensions
of human life.

As in the case of Protestantism, we can find a positive
side to modern social theory, remnants of the *communio*
mentality. I hinted earlier that the ferocity of Hobbes was
mitigated by Locke. What softened things was Locke's conviction that God exists, that human beings are creatures, and
that their rights are therefore not simply functions of desire but correlates of their dignity. This Lockean shift can be
seen in Jefferson's insistence that the basic political rights of
Americans are "endowed by their creator." In an evangelical

framework, the dignity of the individual is grounded in the nonviolent and generous act of creation, and in the even more abundantly generous act of redemption. My suspicion is that these great Christian motifs appear, in admittedly obscured form, in Locke, Jefferson, and the best of the modern rights tradition. John Paul II confirms this in speech after speech, insisting that a culture of life must be predicated upon a respect for individual rights, especially the right of freedom of religion and conscience.

Another overtone of the *communio* harmony can be found in the American experiment in law-governed pluralism. From the earliest days, Americans knew that their society had to be formed from a wide, almost wild, diversity of religions, cultures, languages, and social styles. Accordingly, they appreciated the central importance of law, dialogue, tolerance, and civil conversation. Without these disciplining and unifying practices, diversity would devolve in very short order into violence. When he came to Chicago in 1979, John Paul II spoke to a typically American audience of tremendous diversity. Looking over the crowd, he reminded them of the beauty of the national motto *e pluribus unum* and suggested that there is a spirituality undergirding that sentiment. The church of Christ is destined to gather into its fold all the peoples of the world, for the Lord commissioned his disciples to "preach the good news to all nations." Therefore, the forging of unity out of diversity — *communio, e pluribus unum* — is an ecclesial as well as social mandate. Indeed, the pope seemed to indicate that in the American experiment in liberal democracy an echo of the church's *communio* can be heard. This insight is especially important given the fact that some evangelizers would want to romanticize the political arrangements in place during the Middle Ages or some other period of supposed Catholic ascendancy. While remaining detached from any and all particular social systems, the church can find evangelical analogues and correspondences in classical, medieval, or modern political forms.

Thus, the one who would sow the seed of the kerygma in the context of the American culture confronts both stony and fertile ground. She faces a society that is, on the one hand, deeply marked by the unraveling of the social and intellectual fabric of *communio*. But on the other hand, she operates within a society that retains hints, overtones, colorings of the paschal mystery. What then, precisely, to do? I should like to propose a series of practices.

The Strangest Way

In the Acts of the Apostles, Christianity is referred to by the evocative phrase "the Way." What this signals is that Christianity is not simply a matter of articulate beliefs and organizational structure, but rather an entire pattern or form of life. In the first chapter of the Gospel of John, we hear Jesus in conversation with two of the Baptist's disciples: "Where do you stay?" they ask him. "Come and see," he responds. Then the narrator tells us that they stayed with him the rest of that day. Only after that sojourn do they proclaim that he is the long-awaited Messiah. The message seems clear: Jesus wants not simply to communicate teachings and insights; he wants to share his life, his way of being; he wants to show them where and how he stays. Just as, in the Middle Ages or Renaissance, an apprentice would move in with a painter, watching his moves and imitating the rhythms of his life long before actually learning the techniques of the art, so the evangelist must move in with the Lord and learn his way before daring to speak of him. When the young Gregory Thaumaturgos came to Origen for instruction in the Christian faith, Origen told him that first he must share the life of the Christian community and only then endeavor to learn the truths of the Creed.

I fear that this understanding of Christianity as a wholly integrated amalgam of thought, passion, movement, gesture,

and practice has become largely attenuated in the modern period. In many of the modern philosophers, a sharp wedge was
driven between body and soul or sensuousness and reason.
When this dichotomy was applied to religion it resulted, as
we have seen, in a valorization of the subjective and interior
dimension and a de-valorization of the objective arena of ritual and practice. The very best example of this tendency is
Kant's *Religion within the Limits of Reason Alone,* wherein
the philosopher argues for a completely subjective/ethical
construal of the faith and recommends the jettisoning of
prayer, liturgy, ecclesial structure, and the particularities of
revelation. We can hear echoes of the modern project in
the dominant theologies of the twentieth century, including
Tillich's and Rahner's, both of which commence with, and
order themselves around, an inner sensibility. And in the popular preaching and theologizing of the past forty years in this
country, the modern style has been in the ascendancy. Think
of the myriad workshops, retreats, and sermons that have
asked us to access a feeling or experience of God, without
relating that experience to a concrete way of life, or judging it
in terms of a revealed tradition. It is my conviction that this
mode of preaching and evangelizing has proven remarkably
counterproductive, especially in an American context that is,
as we have been arguing, so thoroughly and problematically
shaped by the individualism and subjectivism of the modern
period. In fact, it dovetails perfectly with the peace treaty we
described earlier: religion is tolerable as long as it is privatized,
sequestered in the arena of feeling or inner experience.

Accordingly, I propose an evangelistic style that is bold,
public, embodied, and expressed in terms of concrete practices. I desire a Christianity that, in direct opposition to the
terms of the modern peace treaty, shows up. Let us turn
now to a consideration of just a few of these practices that
constitute the distinctive Christian way.

One of the greatest works of medieval literature, *The
Canterbury Tales,* centers around a group of people, in the

rush of springtime enthusiasm, going on pilgrimage. For Europeans of the Middle Ages, there were few activities more important, dangerous, and exciting than pilgrimages. They criss-crossed the continent, from Cologne, to Paris, to Chartres, to Vezelay, to Rome, to Compostela, some even traversing the sea to Jerusalem — in order to look at the relics of saints. Many explanations — economic, political, social — have been forwarded to make sense of this enormous vitality, but at the heart of the matter is faith. Christian life is about movement, for it plays itself out around two basic poles: Jesus' call to conversion and his post-resurrection commission to preach the gospel. We move toward Christ away from sin, and we move toward the world for the sake of proclamation; the one thing we don't do is sit still. Thus, for the medieval mind, the pilgrimage to Compostela or Rome or Jerusalem — with all of its attendant dangers and excitement — was to mimic the demand and adventure of the spiritual path.

Can this practice still be part of the Christian way? Can it be a means to evangelization? In recent years, the pope has revived the custom of the pilgrimage in remarkable style through the celebration of the various World Youth Days. So great a crowd assembled in Paris that young people, joining hands, were able to circle the entire city; the gathering at World Youth Day in Manila constituted, by most accounts, the largest single collection of human beings in history; so many young people gathered at Mile High Stadium in Denver that their cheers literally buffeted the pope's helicopter as it came in for a landing. The attractiveness and spiritual power of this very public practice seem not to have faded. Why couldn't our churches encourage and organize pilgrimages to the National Shrine in Washington, or the tomb of Mother Cabrini in New York, or to Guadalupe in Mexico City, or to one of our great monasteries — St. Meinrad or Gethsemani or Snowmass? Or why couldn't we sponsor marches through our cities and neighborhoods, reclaiming them for Christ, or May crownings and Corpus Christi processions? That all of this strikes many of us as slightly embarrassing is undoubtedly a function of our formation in a privatized religiosity. But an evangelizing church is one that, like it or not, shows up.

During the past forty years or so, we have, in the Catholic world, built beige churches, that is to say, structures that are largely void of symbolism, imagery, iconography, and narrativity. In accord with the subjectivist prejudices of modernity, they are buildings where the pilgrim people of God gather, but not, themselves, narrators of the Christian story. The Gothic cathedrals of the Middle Ages, on the contrary, were not simply tents of meeting, but powerful repositories of Christian symbolism, places that, consequently, *formed* those who entered them and even those who passed by. The distinctiveness of the Christian *communio* metaphysics was on display in the rose windows, the glass, the facades, the orientation of the edifice, the decoration, etc. If our ecclesial buildings are to have an evangelical power, they must not simply blend in with the suburban environment around them or conform to the subjectivist and minimalist aesthetic of the time. Rather, they must be symbolic manifestations (both inside and out) of the understanding of being that flows from the dying and rising of Jesus.

Another central practice of the Christian community is the liturgy. According to the intellectual leaders of the liturgical movement of the last century — Romano Guardini, Odo Casel, Virgil Michel, Reynold Hillenbrand, and others — the liturgy is a sort of iconic display of God's justice or order, an aesthetic showing forth of *communio*. And this is why the Mass, for them, had such a powerful influence in the areas of politics and social organization. Dorothy Day saw this connection during the period of her conversion to the faith. Even with their baroque decoration and arcane liturgical language, the Catholic churches were the places where the common people, the immigrants felt at home, even rubbing shoulders with members of the upper classes. The very way that we gather for the Eucharist, stubbornly compelling everyone to come together despite economic, racial, and cultural differences, constitutes in itself an embodiment of the *communio* form.

We find the same dynamic all throughout the liturgy. The commencement of the ritual proper under the sign of the cross signals the radical orientation of this community toward the Trinitarian love. The readings and homily — in their symbolism and narrativity — open up the surprising world that appears when the true God is Lord. The prayer of the faithful is one of the behavioral implications of *communio*: since we are bound to each other through Christ and in God, we bear each other's burdens, acknowledging that one person's need is everyone's need. Just before the Eucharistic prayer, the song of the angels is invoked. This is designed to align our faltering communion here below with the fully cooperative and nonviolent communion gathered around the throne of God. At the heart of the matter, of course, is the making present of the Son sent by the Father in order to include the universe in the energy of the Trinitarian compassion. After the Eucharistic prayer, the Lord's Prayer is recited or sung: "Thy kingdom come, thy will be done on earth as it is in heaven." Again, as when we joined our voices to those of the angels, we are engaging in an act and prayer of alignment, hoping that the *ordo* of heaven becomes the *ordo* of earth. The most ecstatic part of the liturgy is the eating and drinking of Christ's body and blood, for it is here that the co-inherence of God and creation becomes most intense. We are drawn out of ourselves in order to meet, with some adequacy, the ecstatic gift of self that Christ offers. Finally, it has been said that the most sacred words of the liturgy, after those of the consecration itself, are the words of dismissal: "The Mass is ended; go in peace to love and serve the Lord." Once eucharisticized through all of the ritual, symbolism, and narrativity of the Mass, the community is sent in order to eucharisticize the world, to make densely real the *communio* that they experienced in the liturgy.

In a word, the liturgy at its best is the most intense expression of the *communio* vision and hence the most powerful tool for evangelization. The Mass is Maurin's "dynamite of the church," but too often we domesticate it or secularize it, turning it into a celebration of ourselves. This, above all, robs it of its power to transform the world.

A final practice, or better, set of practices that I would like to recommend are the corporal and spiritual works of mercy. Dorothy Day commented that everything a baptized Christian does should be directly or indirectly related to these concrete, active embodiments of the *communio* attitude: feeding the hungry, clothing the naked, giving drink to the thirsty, visiting those in prison, praying for the living and the dead, comforting the sorrowful, forgiving sinners, etc. Many Christians would gladly claim that they are proponents of peace and justice, but without sufficiently specifying those abstractions. After all, every political philosopher from Plato to Karl Marx advocates some form of peace and justice. The corporal and spiritual works compel one to incarnate and instantiate those forms in a properly Christian manner and context. Because we are connected to one another as creatures and in Christ, because we participate in the primal *communio* of the divine persons, we must care for the needs of the brothers and sisters. Because we co-inhere in one another, we can never perceive one person's suffering as uniquely his own; rather, we must claim his hunger or thirst or loneliness as our own.

A few years ago, an article appeared in the *New York Times* focusing on the difference between priests ordained in the 1960s and priests being ordained today. While the older generations of clergy were eager to be on the streets, working directly with the poor and disadvantaged, fighting for social justice, the younger clerics, it seemed, were content to remain in the sanctuary, concentrating their energy and attention on liturgy, prayer, and contemplation. The burden of the article was that this was an evolution much to be regretted. To my mind, what is to be regretted is the wedge that was driven between street and sanctuary in the years after the Vatican Council. For Dorothy Day — who attended daily Mass, recited the rosary, went on frequent retreats, prayed unceasingly — the link between contemplation of the divine mystery and the most radical work on behalf of the poor was perfectly obvious. Her practical mission grew organically out of her intense concentration upon the sacred *communio* — and this gave it, of course, its enormous evangelical power. She saw that the church, giving visible witness to its belief in co-inherence, would have a transforming effect throughout the society.

Conclusion

I should like to close by returning to a key question that I raised at the outset, namely, how can the evangelical message be proclaimed non-coercively in the context of a free and pluralistic society? What I hope has become clear in the course of this discussion is that the *communio* message is essentially a word of nonviolence. In the paschal mystery, the first Christians saw that the deepest meaning of the real is peace, compassion, forgiveness, connection. Therefore, to proclaim the Christian message in a coercive, manipulative, arrogant, or violent way is to fall into a sort of practical contradiction. But non-coerciveness by no means implies reticence, indifference, or non-publicness. Catholics eager to evangelize the American scene ought to know clearly who they are and ought to act visibly out of that identity. Richard Rohr has commented that at the heart of the enlightened liberal project is the conviction that cruelty is the primal moral problem, and from this he concludes that the essential public responsibility of the state is to foster inclusiveness and toleration. A Christian, it seems to me, might agree quite readily that cruelty is the sin of sins, but he ought not to conclude that something as bland as toleration is the solution. Instead, the Christian ought to propose that cruelty is best countered by love, *communio,* nonviolence — practices that flow from the paschal mystery of Jesus crucified and risen from the dead. These concrete gestures are, at the same time, deeply Christian and positively transformative in the context of a liberal, pluralist society. When believers instantiate them boldly and unapologetically, they work, as the gospel parable has it, like a leaven within a society compromised by the breakdown of *communio.*

Chapter Ten

BEYOND RESILIENCE
TO RENAISSANCE

A Canadian Case Message
for Catholics Everywhere

Reginald W. Bibby

R OMAN CATHOLICISM in Canada represents a significant
religious anomaly. On the plus side, the church is having
more success than any other religious group in the country
when it comes to retaining its own people intergenerationally.
However, on the minus side, the church has experienced a
sharp decline in attendance over the past forty years. Contrary to common interpretations, the research suggests that
such a decline has not been some kind of inevitable result
of social and culture change whereby Catholics have become
indifferent to the church. The participation drop-off is rather
primarily the result of a failure of ministry. Catholicism in
Canada is currently faced with a harsh reality that is calling
for a concerted response: significant numbers of Catholics
are not finding the church to be in touch with their spiritual, personal, and relational needs. But there are signs that
just such an improved response is taking place in some parts
of the country, leading to a modest increase in attendance
nationwide.

What's taking place in Canada is hardly unique to Canada. The downs and ups of the Catholic Church there may serve as a helpful and instructive prototype for the church's activities in many other countries, starting with the United States.

A Few Important Facts

Let me elaborate a bit. The old adage of "once a Catholic, always a Catholic" continues to hold in Canada, as does the idea that "Catholics beget Catholics." Some nine in ten people who were raised in Roman Catholic homes continue to view themselves as Catholics, compared to a level of just under eight in ten for mainline and conservative Protestants. What's intriguing is that most of the remaining one in ten people with Catholic parents do not defect to other groups. The vast majority are younger adults who describe themselves as having "no religion"; one in three of Canada's "religious nones" come from Catholic homes. However, the category is frequently a temporary residence. Within five years, approximately one in three of these same Catholic offspring move out and "re-identify" themselves as Catholics, a figure that increases to two in three within ten years. Such a psychological return to the Catholic fold is directly related to people pursuing rites of passage relating to marriage, the arrival of children, and the death of family members. The facts of the matter add up to a situation where the overwhelming majority of people who come from Catholic parentage in Canada either never leave home or leave and then return. To borrow a sports analogy, the Catholic Church may drop the second and third games; but in the case of most people, it comes back to win the best-of-seven series.

There's no doubt about it: across generations, most Catholics remain Catholics. To be sure, many and perhaps a majority are into religion à la carte, attending infrequently, commonly disagreeing with teachings in areas such as sexuality and the role of women in the church. Their confidence in leaders fluctuates in the face of incompetence and immorality. But Catholics they remain. One wonders who is more surprised — Catholic leaders or the religious competition, in both instances making the common mistake of equating lack of involvement with religious defection. The "identification without involvement" pattern in Canada was summed up a few years back by one church leader with words that are particularly applicable to "latent" Catholics: "It's not that they're leaving; it's just that they're not coming."

And so it is that as the twenty-first century began, almost one in two of Canada's 30 million people viewed themselves as Roman Catholics — easily outnumbering any other religious category, including mainline (20 percent) and evangelical Protestants (8 percent). Some 6 million Catholics resided in Quebec, about 7 million in the rest of the country. However, only about one in four of these 13 million Catholics were attending Mass on a weekly basis, with the level lower in Quebec (20 percent) than elsewhere (32 percent).

Catholics and National Trends

Given the numerical dominance of Roman Catholics in Canada, national attendance trends can be expected to ebb and flow in accordance with the ups and downs of Catholic attendance. Since the 1960s, the trend has been largely ebb in both instances.

In the United States, Gallup has found that weekly service attendance across the nation has remained fairly steady at around 45 percent since the mid-1970s, even though Catholics have experienced a slight attendance drop-off. A good empirical case can be made for the fact that the primary reason for such stability is that losses for Catholics who comprise about one-quarter of the population have been offset by slight increases among Protestant groups as a whole who make up one-half of the population. The Protestants have been led by evangelicals, notably Baptists and large independent congregations.

However, in Canada, just the opposite situation has occurred. Numerically dominant Catholics literally dragged down the national service attendance level in the post-1960s. Between 1975 and 2000, weekly attendance across Canada dropped from 31 percent to 21 percent, but not because of the Protestants. For all the publicity given the decline of mainline Protestant numbers, Protestant weekly attendance during the period remained steady at about 25 percent. The falling mainline numbers were offset by conservative Protestant increases. One is left with one fairly obvious deduction: Canada's attendance decline in the post-1960s was due primarily to the fact that Catholic attendance fell from 45 percent in 1975 to 27 percent in 2000.

In the early years of the new century, there are signs that organized religion in Canada is making a comeback — that something of an embryonic renaissance of organized religion could be occurring. There have been increases in participation among teenagers and young adults, with these increases starting to be reflected in overall national attendance figures. A Gallup poll conducted in late 2004 found that national monthly-plus attendance was the highest it has been since the early 1980s. Consistent with that finding, my own latest national survey completed in late 2005 revealed that between 2000 and 2005 national weekly attendance increased from about 20 percent to 25 percent — representing the first increase in almost five decades.

Whether the increase in participation is merely a blip on the pollster's screen or a sign of something much greater will depend in large measure on the Catholic Church, and how it responds to its own people. In global context, what "the Canadian microcosmic case" suggests is how the church responds to its 1 billion people around the world will have much to say, not only about the vitality of Catholicism, but also about the impact of the Christian faith on the entire planet.

Catholic Resilience

The resilience of Catholicism in Canada and many other countries has been nothing less than remarkable. While social scientists dating back to Emile Durkheim and Karl Marx saw the Catholic Church as in an irreversible state of demise, developments to date have proven them wrong. Countries around the world that historically have been predominantly Catholic continue to be predominantly Catholic. Identification with Catholicism has remained entrenched, even if participation and commitment have been called into question. It is difficult to think of any significant exceptions to such a historical rule.

In Canada, for example, the first national census in 1871 found that 42 percent of Canadians viewed themselves as Roman Catholics. As of the latest census in 2001, the figure stood at 43 percent. Incidentally, during the same 130-year period, the proportion of the population who identified with conservative Protestant, evangelical groups remained steady at 8 percent, while those identifying with other world faiths increased modestly from 2 percent to 6 percent. Most of the balance identified themselves as mainline Protestants or indicated they had no religion — with considerable life-stage-related movement taking place between the two categories.

Over time, Catholics in particular have shown extreme reluctance to try just any religious supplier. Asked bluntly in 2000 if they were open to the possibility of switching to another religious tradition supplier, about eight in ten Canadians said no. In Quebec, to no one's surprise, 98 percent of weekly attending Roman Catholics said the door to such a possibility was closed. The eye-opener was that the "no" figure for Quebec Catholics who attend services less than once as week was 97 percent.

These kinds of findings make it clear that Roman Catholicism continues to be the dominant player on the Canadian religious scene — part of a powerful, long-established multi-national religious corporation with considerable organizational strength and significant recuperative powers. Contrary to the ongoing prophecies of its demise in the face of everything from secularization to scandal, Catholicism remains a part of the lives of millions of Canadians. The church loses fairly small numbers to other groups and knows a steady stream of additions as Catholics migrate to Canada from various parts of the world. It all adds up to a remarkably high level of resilience for the church as an organization, and for the Catholic faith at the level of individuals. It also is not a situation that is about to change.

The Great Opportunity

What for many observers is somewhat stunning about the situation with Catholics is that large numbers who are not actively involved report that they are anything but indifferent or hostile. A number of our recent national surveys have asked people who attend services less than once a month if they would consider the possibility of being more involved in a religious group if they found it to be worthwhile for themselves or their families. More than one in two Canadians have indicated that they are receptive to greater participation — with Catholic numbers in Quebec and elsewhere virtually identical to the national figure.

The obvious and crucial question, of course, is what would Catholics see as "worthwhile." We have followed up the initial inquiry about receptivity by pointedly asking, "What kind of things would make it worthwhile?" The dominant response? Ministry. Catholics say that they would be open to greater involvement in parishes that could help them address their spiritual needs. Many indicate what all of us know well — that people are finding life tough and would be receptive to a church that could provide them with some help and sustenance as they try to cope with their difficulties. Large numbers report that their marriages are not going all that well, or that they are having difficulty raising their children — sometimes that they simply want to make sure their children turn out all right. If they could get some help with these centrally important family issues, then, "Yes," they would be open to greater involvement. The second most prevalent response after ministry? People say they are looking for changes in the way that the church carries out ministry. They indicate they are open to greater involvement in parishes that speak to life as they are living it, respect diversity, are more contemporary, are a little less dogmatic, and, frankly, more positive and more life-giving.

In short, the research suggests that the key to Canadians generally and Roman Catholics specifically becoming more involved in churches does not lie with merely getting people to attend services. The key lies in doing what Jesus did — ministering to their needs. We now have mounds of data that corroborate what we all know: to the extent that people find significance in churches — find that faith and churches touch their lives — they want to have more to do with faith and churches.

Simply put, Canadians readily indicate that they have spiritual interests and needs, are experiencing various problems and challenges as they live out everyday life, and value good relationships more than anything else — beginning with family life. Churches that can touch their lives and the lives of their families spiritually, personally, and relationally are churches to which they will be drawn. In short, Canadians are open to churches that have a significant place in their lives. That's when involvement is worth their time and their resources.

The Great Responsibility

Through the eyes of the believer, the evidence indicates that God has been at work in Canadian lives. God is still expecting a lot from Canada's churches. Given that almost one in two Canadians continue to see themselves as Catholics, there is no way of avoiding a blatant conclusion: at this point in history, God is expecting a lot of the Roman Catholic Church.

One could sidestep that conclusion if the rumors that are rampant in the media, church circles, and even academic circles were accurate: if Catholics in Quebec and elsewhere no longer saw themselves as Catholics, if people who were baptized Catholic were defecting to other groups and having their needs met in other places, if Catholics just sat at home on Sundays and were not receptive to greater involvement.

But the rumors are false. Catholics, whether they show up lots or show up little, continue to see themselves as Catholics. The vast majority are not "religious free agents" who are casing out other groups. And the clincher is that they are telling the Catholic Church that they are receptive to greater involvement — if that involvement can touch their lives in meaningful ways.

So is that it? Is all well? Can the church just sit back and relax? Not at all. It never has been the role of the sheep to find the shepherd. Given the reluctance of Catholics to turn elsewhere, there is good reason to believe that if the Catholic Church fails to reach inactive Catholics, those people are not going to be reached by anyone.

For the sociologist who is looking on, what needs to happen is pretty obvious. To the extent that the Catholic Church is serious about evangelization, it has a mandate to do what no other group in the country can do, namely, get serious about targeting Roman Catholics. I run into a large number of religious leaders who continue to want to treat "what's required next" as a great mystery or as something that calls for magical kinds of solutions. They think there is a need to wander around the wilderness in order to "discern" what they should do next. Or they are looking for what amounts to "magic potions" that will miraculously transform their parishes.

In my mind, at this point in history, there is no need to treat the methodology required as either particularly complex or mysterious, and certainly not as something that is magical. In straightforward terms, the church needs to make contact with Catholics who are on the fringe of parish life, engage them in conversations concerning their interests and needs, and then, as parishes are able, minister to them.

Beyond Canada

If much of this sounds familiar to readers in other countries where a Catholic presence is significant, it should. Catholics typically know a high level of success in continuing to create Catholics intergenerationally. Research and polls around the world confirm what Catholics in any number of national settings know firsthand: identification readily persists; defection is relatively limited and often not lifelong. Latent Catholics frequently surface when key events relating to marriage, birth, and death take place. Considerable picking and choosing goes on, participation is not necessarily high, commitment is often fairly low.

But Catholics tend to stay Catholics who in turn beget Catholics who repeat the cycle. When is involvement more extensive, commitment more intense? We all know It seems so obvious that it hardly should have to be underlined — but it needs to be underlined for those who insist on treating the sources of involvement and commitment as elusive mysteries. We give our lives — our time, our money — to those things that we define as significant. Faith and church involvement are no different. Commitment and parish involvement follow when people come to define the faith and the church as touching their lives in significant ways.

This is not merely the case in Canada; the Canadian case has applicability worldwide.

Roman Catholics in Canada have before them an extraordinary opportunity. The research shows that, contrary to widespread propaganda, Canada is far from a "godless" country. On the contrary, the believer is left with the inescapable conclusion that God has been at work, preparing people, relating to them, and awakening them. It's as if God has sometimes grown impatient with the churches and decided to show up in Person. I'm not exaggerating. Some eight in ten Canadians not only believe in God but believe in a God who cares about them personally. Approximately the same number say they are talking to God at least occasionally, five in ten at least once a week. Not surprisingly, given such belief and prayer realities, some five in ten also maintain that they themselves have experienced God's presence. God is doing extremely well in the polls. What is needed now is for parishes and individuals to respond to all this preparatory work, starting with their own people — some 13 million of them.

Similarly, in Catholic settings around the world, there is a great need for the church to assess how well it is ministering to Catholics, reaching out to its own people versus waiting and even demanding that "the sheep find the shepherd." One prominent Catholic leader recently suggested to me that the fact Catholics assume that their people remain Catholics can lull the church into complacency. It knows it has the sheep somewhere in the big fenced field, and therefore doesn't feel any particular rush to go out and find them and feed them. Obviously that outlook has to change. One Protestant observer I also spoke with recently was less charitable: he suggested that in many parishes, the idea of taking the initiative to go after the sheep is right off the Catholic radar screen. He probably doesn't know what he's talking about. You be the judge.

As I understand it, the Catholic Church at its highest levels speaks of the urgency that needs to characterize finding Catholics and ministering to them. For example, in the church's Directory for Catechesis, released by the Vatican in 1997, normal forms of evangelism were acknowledged as important. However, specific attention was also given to Catholic adults who were described as being "in need of different types of Christian formation" — people being in what was referred to as "an intermediate situation." The Directory for Catechesis put it this way:

> [Here] entire groups of the baptized have lost a living sense of the faith, or even no longer consider themselves members of the Church and live a life far removed from Christ & his Gospel. Such situations require "a new evangelization."

To the extent that Catholics everywhere have been letting many of their people "slip between the cracks," the time has come for high priority to be given to locating them and responding to them.

No one is saying it is going to be easy. For one thing, Catholics in many settings, including North America, are short on both churches and priests. In Canada, the ratio for Catholics of churches to people is approximately 1:2,000, compared to 1:280 for evangelical Protestants. As for parish priests, Canada has about 1 priest for every 1,600 Catholics, compared to a ratio of 1:200 for evangelicals.

Those kinds of church and priest shortages are showing. Our surveys have found that when active Roman Catholics have faced serious problems, no less than 63 percent, two in three, say that the church wasn't even aware of what they were going through — more than double the 28 percent figure for Protestants. It means that the laity are going to have to play a key role in all this. But somehow, in Canada and elsewhere, ways have to be found to locate Catholics, to ask them if they are okay, and to seek to minister to them.

As noted earlier, there are signs that such a response is indeed becoming more widespread in Canada, to date primarily outside Quebec. During the 1990s, the proportion of adults under thirty-five who attended weekly stopped plunging for the first time in decades. In addition, perhaps spurred on by Pope John Paul II's declaration in the 1980s that "youth are the hope of the Church," Catholics joined evangelical Protestants and many other religious groups in accelerating their efforts to minister to young people, complete with full-time and part-time youth ministry specialists. The result has been a post-1980s upturn in teenage attendance. Such developments among Catholics, combined with Protestant revitalization efforts and the vitality of many other faith groups, has contributed to modest increases in national attendance.

Today Roman Catholics in Canada are facing a great opportunity. In the light of the size of their constituency, Catholics also are facing a great responsibility. Very similar situations exist in other countries, beginning with the United States. Some very significant things can happen. Moreover, they must happen. "To whom much has been given, much is expected." Catholics potentially have much to bring. They need to come through, and thereby go well beyond resilience to playing a major role in the renaissance of Christian faith. The final lines of *Restless Gods* (p. 248) can be expanded to refer not merely to one country but to what is taking place and what could take place worldwide:

> To look at Canada in the first decade of the new
>   millennium
> is to see a country characterized by religious restlessness.
> The churches are restless. Canadians are restless.
> It may well be because, "in the beginning" of this new
>   century,
> the "Spirit of God which moved upon the face of the
>   waters" back then
> is moving across the country.
> What remains to be seen is what will be created . . . this
>   time around.

Discussion Questions

In reflecting with Roman Catholic leaders on my research findings and ministry implications, I have posed a number of questions that I think need to be raised if effective ministry to people on the edges of Catholic life is ever going to take place. Here are some of them for your information and possible use.

1. In general, do you know who your less active people are?

2. Does your parish have ways of "cataloging" strangers who attend services?

3. Can people in your parish be motivated to engage in ministry to less involved Catholics?

4. Be honest — are you waiting for the sheep to come to you?

5. How do you feel about mega-parishes with multiple staff members being established?

6. In your parish, how can "the caseload" be better shared?

7. What can parishes do to cultivate a better awareness of the personal needs of members?

8. Is it possible for your parishes and schools to work together more closely to ensure that both young people and families are ministered to more effectively?

9. Many people say they are receptive to greater involvement that they find to be worthwhile. Could it be that there are sizable numbers of Catholics, both active and less active, who similarly are open to greater financial involvement if they found the ministry causes — such as ministry to children and teenagers — to be worthwhile?

10. Do you have a person or people with whom you are able to reflect on the activity of God in your life, and in the life of your parish?

Chapter Eleven

EVANGELIZATION IN SECULARITY

Fishing for People in the Oceans of Culture

Ronald Wayne Young, O.M.I.

Jesus said to them, "Come after me, and I will make you fishers of men." Then they abandoned their nets and followed him. (Mark 1:17–18)

W E SWIM in the vast ocean that is culture. This ocean of culture is everything that is not biologically determined about us. It may well be that the fact that we exist as creatures of culture is in itself a biological determination, a part of the divine design. Nevertheless, culture is the mother of all that there is to learn. It defines us as creatures who hunger to know and, in knowing of ourselves and the world around us, to become more than we have been individually and collectively.

Tremendous is culture's power to obscure as well as reveal. We swim in culture's ocean often frightened, confused, and full of self-doubt, toward an ultimate reality that it seems we cannot easily perceive along the way. All that is our culture communicates a pathway to living or a pathway to dying that is set before us as a choice. Within the vast ocean of our culture it is a hard, but necessary fact that we have to choose what path we will follow. This is the essential "learning curve" of the dualities of our existence: life or death, good or evil, mutual creativity or self-destruction.

What we call secularity is a defining aspect of the modern culture which we inhabit. Essentially, secularity is a point of view. To live in the moment, to "seize the day," to entertain the actualities of what can be perceived by the senses and interpreted within the framework of its own meaning is secularity. It is an affirmation of actualities and potentialities that can be readily described, mastered, and achieved within this present space and time.

Sources of Secularity

The nature of modern secular consciousness begins, in one sense, with the nature of being human. It has to do with a relationship to worldly or temporal affairs as distinct from spiritual considerations. Early Persian Zoroastrian religious and Greek philosophical conceptions of the duality in the contrasting relationship between temporal and spiritual matters resulted in dualism, imposing an absolute division between these experiences. Awareness of the present moment of time and the timeless moment of presence, a utilitarian purpose for space and a sacred space providing purpose were often conceived with a strict division.

Secularity emerged into political and social life with Confucius (551–479 BC) who proposed a system of moral behavior that was essentially secular in China. Around the same time, the democracies of ancient Greece (600–400 BC) flourished in secular splendor. Both are secular in the sense that their basis was not divine injunction and their goals were not otherworldly. However, their experience and the modern experience of secularity differ drastically in relation to the attitude toward religion.

Sociologists tell us that the modern cultural phenomenon of secularization is "generated" by the interplay of traditional Western cultural elements with scientific developments and their accompanying philosophical foundations. In this sense, we live in post-Christian, post-ecclesial cultures since Christianity and its church are central aspects of Western civilization. Thus, as children of post-Enlightenment cultures, we have assumed consciously and unconsciously the rhetoric of the sciences and the humanities over the previous Judeo-Christian myth-narrative of Western civilization.

Confronted with mystery, we answer that it is only a matter of time until what is true is revealed through the application of the scientific method. Our secularized sense of truth is observable, describable, predictable, controllable, and repeatable. Everything that is presently beyond our grasp is either to be conquered by science or discarded as extraneous data derived from questionable observation. Myth is equated with fiction rather than providing the large-scale truths under which smaller-scale systems operate. Thus, secularized truth is an accumulation of small truths that eventuate in the postulation of grand general theories of how "life, the universe, and everything" function.

Disseminating Secularity

Secularity is exported by the ever developing technologies of travel and communication. The relative sophistication of these two factors is directly related to the scope of secularity's influence. From traveling on foot to riding a horse, from riding a horse to journeying by wagon, from wagon train to automobile ride, from auto to propeller plane flight, from propeller plane to jet, travel speeds up. From communicating the news by town crier to written parchment, from written parchment to newspaper, from newspaper to Internet, the means of communication develop in precision. Each development allows for the rapid dissemination of new ideas and technologies.

The power of technology for good or ill is magnified by speedier systems of travel and more precise systems of communication leading to the homogenization of local cultures into a globalized culture. Globalization is not in every way bad, except where it leads to the domination of less-developed cultures by more technologically sophisticated ones for the purpose of mere economic gain. Globalization also has the potential to go a long way to solving the worldwide problems of hunger, disease, and poverty.

Good News and Bad News

All culture is formed and fashioned with positive and negative traits. It seems that our cultures bear the values and virtues as well as the blinders and disabilities of their human inhabitants. At its best, secularity serves to invite us into the present reality, to take hold of our lives, our communities, our societies, and our world, to form and fashion them in our image and likeness and to see the beauty of our artistry reflected, as in a mirror, as the fruit of our handiwork.

At its worst, secularity sets us adrift to the forces of our own limitations. Seeking to be logical, practical, and realistic, we enter into the utilitarian meaninglessness of this moment when disconnected with the accumulation and culmination of all moments. Enamored with the present, we journey among the details of life while overlooking the bigger picture. We become those who "cannot see the forest for the trees," and in this we lose a realistic view of ourselves in relation to a living spirituality that leads to God.

Secularity is an awareness of "here-ness" as compared to "there-ness." However, while the dualities of existence have traditionally been perceived in such a way as to authenticate the mystery of being, secularity often devolves to become a servant of dualism. Thus, the secular and the sacred can become opponents in a tug-of-war between our present realities and future potentialities. This is secularism. It can become a

faith in the present over the past and the future. It is either
this or that with secularism; there can be no middle ground,
no nexus of meaning that leads us beyond self-awareness to
other-awareness and from other-awareness to God-awareness.

We can become lost to temporal and spatial narcissism in
the vast ocean of culture, to see ourselves, our present, our
limitations and struggles as ends in themselves. Secularism
can lead to a

> ...vicious circle: when the sense of God is lost, there
> is also a tendency to lose the sense of man, of his dig-
> nity and his life; in turn, the systematic violation of the
> moral law, especially in the serious matter of respect for
> human life and its dignity, produces a kind of progres-
> sive darkening of the capacity to discern God's living
> and saving presence. (*Evangelium Vitae*, 21)

In this, John Paul II suggests that we have moved from a "culture of life" to a "culture of death" due to a faith in the present
over a faith in the One who provides the present.

Discerning the Mission in Secularity

Among people there seems to be a measure of confusion regarding the intimacy of God with the world that God made.
Often enough, the question is about where holiness resides.
Is God helping only the saved or striving for the well-being
of everyone, even in the most secularized contexts? Is the
Holy Spirit's concern circumscribed by the project of attending exclusively to "holy" people or of developing a sense of
the sacred in all people? How near God is to the world and,
consequently, how near must missionaries be to the world of
God's concern is a most important issue.

It is at the call of the mission to reach the world effectively
with the gospel that compels the church to adapt itself, without betraying the divine mission and the prophetic message of
the Missionary Lord whom it serves. This has most recently

been called "inculturation." In the context of secularity, this raises the question, What adaptations of the church will best serve the needs of the mission given the culture of secularity? Paraphrasing H. Richard Niebuhr in his work *Christ and Culture*, there are basically three ways we may respond to secularized culture.

We may take the view of "Christ against culture," that an appropriate distance from secularity is needed. This is the position that Christian fidelity rejects loyalty to cultural convention where they disagree. This means prophetically living the radical nature of the gospel, to awaken people to the fact that religion is not simply a tool of culture, but a revelation about the true nature of existence that is beyond the confines of cultural circumscription.

Alternatively, the church may attempt an accommodation, so that differences are minimized and alignments emphasized in favor of a "Christ of culture" — drawing near to secularity for the sake of effective communication and religious understanding by adopting a medium and language suited to the context. In this way, the church usurps the powerful forces of cultural symbol and logic to re-present the gospel as a relevant way of life.

Then again, we may choose the path of "Christ above culture." This is the idea that the universality of Christ transcends every cultural definition. This relationship to culture leads to a clarity of the expression of faith focused upon a narrow course of action that delineates a strong communal identity. Many of the movements present in the church are effective at attracting people and fulfilling their mission because they follow this view of their relationship with culture.

Against, accommodating, or above secularized culture, gospel truth demands both the seemingly contradictory fidelity to the Christian gospel and effectiveness in evangelical communication as missionary activity. Here is the challenge, to recognize that we exist in an ocean of culture and that one major aspect of that culture is our relationship of comfort/discomfort with secularity and the secularized. The mission is to view the positive contributions of secularity and to celebrate them, while confronting the death-dealing forces of the anti-faith of secularism.

Discerning the Secularized

Just as there are different oceans, some salty, some clear, secularity is different, distinct, and unique in differing cultural contexts. The "environmental" factors of secularity produce a diversity of responses and influence how faith is understood and lived out. It is important to recognize that there are different groups influenced by secularity with differing evangelical "situations" swimming the oceans that are culture (*Redemptoris Missio*, 33).

We may identify people who have never heard or known the gospel message. This population is growing within the secularized societies of the West, especially among the young, and most readily benefits from the use of modern media and new programs of openness and outreach to communicate the gospel.

There are those who experience an adequate Christian formation of ordinary pastoral care and activity that are, nevertheless, consciously and unconsciously secularized. These would benefit from catechetical and post-catechetical instruction tailored to their stages of human development that sensitizes them to the realities of secularism and its consequences.

Third, there is an intermediate group where the "baptized have lost a living sense of the faith, or even no longer consider themselves members of the church, and live a life far removed from Christ and his gospel." This group is growing as well. According to this determination, these require a "new evangelization." These require a reframing of the gospel in both rationale and practice that focuses on the connection of spirituality as a lived expression of religion and that emphasizes the relationship of moral consequences with religious practice. The identification of these distinct groups within the highly secularized context is important in clarifying a distinct evangelical approach appropriate to each situation.

God chooses to save people, not particular cultures. Particular cultures, like empires, pass away, but God remains faithful to the mission of loving communication that transcends cultural limitations. In other words, there is a universal culture of human experience that is not limited by human conception. In this, we may see the self-gift of God poured out into the very character of the creation. This is a self-gift of unchanging Beauty, ultimate Truth, and compassionate Love given expression in every encounter with beauty, truth, and love in daily experience.

Who Evangelizes Whom

The only thing more sublime, more powerful, and, therefore, more pervasive than culture in the sheer magnitude of its presence is the One who laid the ocean and filled its vastness with the abundant Gift of Self. There can be no question whether the beautiful creation reflects the beauty of the Creator. The Psalmist wrote, "The heavens declare the glory of God; the sky proclaims its builder's craft" (Ps. 19:2). St. Paul informs us that God's "invisible attributes of eternal power and divinity have been able to be understood and perceived in what he has made" (Rom. 1:20). God evangelizes through the beauty of nature and the inner nature of all things. However, it is one thing to set the wonder that is nature in motion and another to engage in activity within it.

In accord with the Judeo-Christian tradition, the succession of developing covenantal relationships of salvation history expresses God's continued engagement and saving activity within creation. God has a history, a track record of involvement in creation beginning with the covenants of the Old Testament, culminating in the New Covenant who is Jesus Christ himself. Further, this covenantal engagement continues in the relationship of the Pentecost Spirit and the church as an extension of that commitment to see all things brought to their fullness in the realization of grace. It is the Spirit that renews and leads the church in union with the living sacrament of God who is the Christ (*Lumen Gentium*, 4). In effect, God evangelizes through the proclamation of the truth of divine and human interrelationship.

At the same time, the Spirit continues the mission of Christ in creation by bringing to fruition the seed of God's "image and likeness" within human beings. Borrowing from Eusebius of Caesarea, *Ad Gentes* instructs missionaries to "gladly and reverently lay bare the seeds of the Word which lie hidden among their fellows" (*Ad Gentes*, 11). These "seeds" are to be found wherever people strive "to attain truth, goodness and God himself" (*Redemptoris Missio*, 28). God evangelizes through the inner design of human love expressed in spiritual consciousness and moral conscience. Humanity is by design oriented toward the One who creates, redeems, and sanctifies all things. In every sense it must be understood that it is principally God who was, is, and continues to be engaged in each of these ways and many others. God is the primal and primary missionary.

The intimacy of God with creation and all who live within it is a complete and utter dedication of love. The sacred quality where holiness resides is circumscribed by the boundless boundaries of the Spirit's activity, reaching even into the extremes of highly secularized societies. God speaks prophetically within unparalleled created grandeur — in the mutuality of covenant relationship and in the very design of human self-ness — a message of tender love and compassion. God is speaking even now. Thus, through beauty, truth, and love God builds a bridge between the secular present and the transcendent future.

God's Mission Has a Church

There exists a tremendous presumption in some who call themselves missionaries. Not a few have confused their missions with a kind of co-dependency, as though God were waiting upon them to act to redeem and sanctify the human family. As medicine for this attitude we should ask, Whose permission did God seek to send the Christ through incarnation, to teach through his life, to redeem through his death, or to reward his fidelity with resurrection? Rather, God is evangelizing, awakening dying spirits and "breaking in" upon us in often disturbing ways.

It is we who have been gifted to know ourselves in the light of Christ as self-conscious members of the church who are the fruit of that divine missionary activity. As a result of God's mission, we are co-joined by the Spirit with the loving concerns which move the heart of God to act in favor of humanity. It is God who speaks the saving message which the church expresses and inhabits.

It seems to me that when the question arises, How do we evangelize given the circumstance of secularity? I cannot help but wonder what has separated life in the world of the present from its ultimate goal of life in the eternal. When people say that organized religion does not express their living spirituality, this separation is at the heart of the matter.

This separation and its consequences indicate both the situation *in se* and the importance of a clear missionary effort to reflect, to reconnect, and to renew this vital sense of religious context. After all, these two aspects of human life, the present and the eternal, are meant to complement one another in such a way that they reveal the meaning of their associate by means of contrast and comparison. Perhaps a story would express the interrelationship I am trying to articulate.

"A man was in his living room when there was a knock on the door. When he opened the door, it was a policeman, who informed him that a flood was expected and evacuation was recommended. The Believer exclaimed, 'I am a man of God. God will protect me from danger.' As the flood continued to worsen, he was visited by a state trooper, two firemen in a rowboat, and an emergency helicopter, but each time he said, 'The All-Powerful will protect me from danger.' 'You go on,' he answered. The water continued to rise, and the man drowned. When he got to Heaven, he was really upset. 'I demand that you take me to God at once,' said the guy. He was granted an audience with God. 'Lord,' said the man, 'after a lifetime of devotion to you, why would you forsake me in my hour of need?' God said, 'You idiot, I sent two cops, firemen in a rowboat, and a helicopter to save you.' "

The problem of the man in the flood was a serious type of religious blindness. It was serious in that it resulted in his death. He could not perceive God's activity through secular means; therefore, he could not perceive the salvific sacred either. Can we? Does not the Christian faith give expression to the interpenetrating reality of the sacred in the secular in the mysteries at the core of its belief? Incarnation within the context of the beauty of Creation; the redemption of human honesty in relation to perfection, set against the backdrop of divine compassion; the sanctification of human being, making God present in the present — each indicate the way of the divine mission and the pathways of those who would join this effort.

The fruit of this mission is the church that joins itself to the effort of celebrating God's missionary activity by living and proclaiming the love of God in worship and expressed as the love of neighbor through humble servitude. Thus, the challenge is not for the culture to answer, but it is the challenge of believing that the "in-breaking" of God is continual and continuing. We have much to encourage that is positive in our culture. We have much to condemn as inadequate, misleading, or downright dangerous. But most important to understand is that spiritual enlightenment is both the joy and the burden of the enlightened. Our religious insight and moral conscience must be trained to serve to bring both religious insight and moral conscience into the societies we inhabit.

Who Is a Missionary for Secularity?

Since I am a member of a missionary congregation, a student of Christian mission, and a citizen of the United States, my questions naturally revolve around the nature of the church's mission in highly secularized cultural contexts. This inquiry has within it a number of presuppositions. In accord with *Ad Gentes* 2, it presupposes that missionary activity is an essential and guiding aspect of the nature of the worldwide church. It presupposes the church has no alternative but to evangelize in every context where human beings exist in light of the missionary mandate of the Lord Jesus Christ who sends us (Matt. 28:18–20; Mark 16:15–18; Luke 24:46–49; John 20:21–23). Mission is a primal condition for the church to be itself, in that it exists for this purpose. Finally, it presupposes that the entire missionary effort of the church is initiated and modeled out by Jesus and is inspired and guided by the Spirit of Christ at the behest of the One whom Jesus calls Father. It is a participation in the life and mission of the Trinity of God. Nevertheless, the church's participation in the divine mission is a thing of human beings, interacting, relating, and bringing to tangible sacramental experience the mutuality of the Trinitarian undertaking.

It seems to me that the ecclesial vision of the Second Vatican Council is not yet realized and that the consideration of evangelization in highly secularized contexts is an invitation to further this development. There is an imbalance between the mission of the ordained, who serve by leading; the mission of those who live the vowed life, demonstrating Spirit-inspired holiness; and the mission of the laity, who evangelize through the practice of Christian family and social life. Each of these has a most important role to play in the mission of the church.

The trouble is that when any of the participants is either missing or unaware of their important role in the mission of the church, the others cannot help but compensate inadequately. I recall that when I sprained my right ankle, I compensated by placing greater weight on the left one. This resulted in new sources of pain springing up as I hobbled along. Using St. Paul's image of the body as a metaphor for the Body of Christ, when the feet and the hands are enfeebled, it is difficult to see how the other members of the body can operate effectively (1 Cor. 12).

An example of this confusion and its resulting imbalance may be found precisely in many parishes in the idea of lay "ministry." How often have parishioners been honored or rewarded by becoming lectors, extraordinary Eucharistic ministers, directors of religious education, ushers, or choir members by the pastor suggesting that by doing these things they fulfill their "ministry"? Rather than create Eucharistic communities of dynamic interchange between parish life and social or civic life, many times we have created "ministries" that happen exclusively at Sunday Eucharist. They end at the church doors and never reach the secular street where they are most needed.

Are not the most important Christian "ministries" of the laity found in their families, at their jobs, out in the world? Have we then set internal ecclesial "ministry" against external ecclesial mission, reinforcing the separation between the sacred and the secular? It seems to me that it is precisely our "out in the world" missionary practice that must define whatever we might name a ministerial call. In this sense, there needs to be a reaffirmation of the missionary character of all the baptized for the sake of honest effectiveness in highly secularized contexts.

Mission of the Laity in Secularity

The mission to evangelize in every cultural context is a call to all the baptized persons in the church to celebrate the positive aspects and redeem the negative aspects of cultures as well as individuals. This is, at its heart, the priestly, prophetic, and kingly ministry of the People of God who are, at one in the same time, people in the world. The mission of the laity is essential to the effort of evangelizing in the cultures of secularity. According to the Second Vatican Council, it is precisely the role of laypeople in the church to recognize their position and power in family life and local communities as well as the national and international stage, where issues related to secularity are played out.

After acknowledging the important ministerial contributions of the ordained and those who live the vowed life, it is precisely the laity who are characterized by the secular nature of their lives (*Lumen Gentium*, 31). It is the most important thing that sets them apart in the communion of the church in terms of the context where they live and, therefore, in the specific missionary expression of their baptismal vocation. The secular context is a defining element of their "condition and mission" (*LG*, 30). It is the "special way" they "make the Church present and operative in those places and circumstances where only through them can it become the salt of the earth" (*LG*, 33).

It is precisely by "engaging" in temporal affairs and "ordering them according to the plan of God" (*LG*, 31) that the mission of the laity fulfills its vocation to seek the kingdom of God in the world. They are to "work for the sanctification of the world from within as a leaven" (*LG*, 31). It is their "special task to order and to throw light upon these affairs in such a way that they may come into being and then continually increase according to Christ to the praise of the Creator and the Redeemer" (*LG*, 31).

This call to mission is given a heightened sense of urgency in societies that attempt to "build a society with no regard whatever for religion, and which attacks and destroys the religious liberty of its citizens" (*LG*, 36). Since the temporal sphere is governed by its own principles, the laity is called into missionary action "so that the mission of the Church may correspond more fully to the special conditions of the world today" (*LG*, 36). In other words, the first "missionaries" to secularity are the laity because of their natural connection to the secular social, political, economic, educational, and artistic life.

The Vowed Life and the Mission in Secularity

It seems to me that the second-level "missionaries" to secularity are those who live the vowed life. Acknowledging the radical nature of the baptismal call, it is important to recognize the unique potential contributions of those pastoral agents whose Spirit-led charism moves them to take up missionary activity in a formal way. Vowed priests, sisters, and brothers each offer their specific Spirit-inspired charism to educate, to serve the poor, to heal the infirm, or to proclaim the gospel.

Through their living witness to holiness of life expressed through missionary zeal and its resulting communal relationship, they articulate the radical alternative gospel lifestyle of those "in the world, but not of the world." In this, they prophetically serve as a countersign to the worldly values of self-serving humanism, self-indulgence, and ever grasping materialism.

Vows of poverty, chastity, and obedience voiced for the sake of the kingdom of heaven contradict the materialism, exploitation, and grasping for power that seem to characterize the secularism of the present age. They redeem the worst of secularism by modeling and proclaiming a living faith in the situations of daily life. As disciples of the discipline of Christ, they serve as shepherds of the church's holiness, educating by example in the ways of God.

Diversity of expression among communities of religious is a positive sign of the Spirit's overflowing diffusion in reaching out to the world of human suffering and struggle. They offer an essential living witness to the truth that God is present at the heart of the human experience. Because of their diversity, the vowed are able to staff a wide array of programs of training and movements of renewal that educate and encourage the mission of the church in secularity through the mission of the laity.

The Ordained and the Mission in Secularity

A tremendous challenge and an exciting prospect for those who share in the sacrament of orders is precisely how to turn administrative centers where people come for sacramental services into equally impressive centers of outreach and evangelization. This challenge is magnified by the popular expectation that the rectory or parish office is the place to get every kind of help and that Father is there to meet every need that is brought to his attention.

It seems that people often come with the unrealistic expectation that priests are able to function in an impossibly wide-ranging diversity of roles as pastor of souls, psychologist, social worker, teacher, effective preacher on Sundays, and miracle worker. It seems as if more and more is being laid upon people trained and ordained to offer spiritual and pastoral care. Is this really how the Christian mission was intended to be lived out? Isn't the sense of Christian mission better voiced as a shared and mutual expression of the Trinitarian nature of being Christian?

It is in the very nature of the sacrament of holy orders that bishops, priests, and deacons serve the ministry of Christian leadership by leading the ministry of Christian service. They bear the administrative responsibility for the discernment and implementation of the church's mission in the ordinary pastoral situation. In this context, it is important to note that John Paul II includes ordinary pastoral care as one of the missionary "situations" of the church, the implication being that there can be no sense of "ordinary" with reference to pastoral care if the missionary dimension is missing. Just as the missionary character of the universal church is essential to its nature, the missionary dimension of pastoral care that trains and empowers believers for mission is essential to the church's practice.

Given the realities of limited time, space, and personnel resources, what must those responsible to lead do in terms of mission in secularity? In many ways, it is a question of time and resource management. Let's say for argument's sake that the ministry of the church may be divided into four elements: liturgy and prayer, catechetics, community organizing, and Christian service. It is actually far more complex than this. Many focus their attention on liturgy as "The Thing" the church does, leaving all the others as secondary priorities or hoped-for results. Liturgy is good and holy, it is the very life of the church, but if it fails to result in a community trained and empowered for missionary outreach, the question remains, Was it authentic Christian liturgy or something else? The Apostle James wrote, "Demonstrate your faith to me without works, and I will demonstrate my faith to you from my works" (2:18).

In this case, the lack of something demonstrates as much as the presence of something. Therefore, if mission is the very nature of the church, all and every activity of the church may be evaluated in relation to how it trains and empowers for mission in the world. Again, we must avoid the separation between ministries in the church versus mission in the world. It is precisely the mission of our lives that indicates the ministry of our Christian faith and not the reverse.

Some Conclusions

Evangelization is essentially the proclamation of the good news of Jesus' life, death, and resurrection. We have been involved in reflecting on what it means to evangelize with secularity as a cultural given, an important part of the ocean in which we swim. Without fight, flight, or surrender, those who believe that God has that "certain something" to offer without which life is not quite what it is meant to be will identify with the missionary struggle to live and love as God lives and loves.

After all, what does it mean to say that one loves God with all one's knowledge, will, and strength but never says a word about God? If these were fiancés who said they were in love and one of the partners never said a word about the other to their friends and family, wouldn't that be a suspicious kind of love? Would you recommend these two for marriage? The greatest love of neighbor is precisely to share the secret of what enriches and enlivens the whole experience of living. Nevertheless, as every Christian neophyte quickly discovers, the sharing must be in a way people can receive or it will be ineffective or, worse, off-putting.

Thus, the entire church is missionary when oriented by the Spirit and aligned with the missionary Jesus Christ. Nevertheless, following the example of Jesus, Spirit-inspired ecclesiological practice both inspires and empowers while addressing human need. Our administrative centers are challenged to be not only places of welcome for the wounded, but sources of sending the mended to offer the world what they have received to those in need.

While the substance of the proclamation cannot change, it must adapt itself to the secular context of the present. To be palatable, it must adapt in language and presentation to the point where it begins to renew the connection between people's practice of spirituality and the religious traditions that originally inspired them. This inner dialogue has to replace the monologue of our culture's dualism between the secular versus the spiritual and the spiritual versus the religious. It must be an authentic transformation that religion really is a habitation for living spirituality capable of dealing with the complex realities of modern living.

In many ways, the mission in secularity invites us to a mature vulnerability in the world of God's concern. As Madeleine L'Engle wrote in *Walking on Water: Reflections on Faith and Art*: "When we were children, we used to think that when we were grown-up we would no longer be vulnerable. But to grow up is to accept vulnerability. . . . To be alive is to be vulnerable." The focus of the pilgrimage of today's missionary is not so much *to* people as it is *with* people. The focus is no longer merely to view the sinful barbarians of a pagan culture in need of saving. In the present, a very real part of evangelization is the appreciation of what is good about a culture as well as the mandate to challenge what is contrary to the gospel.

Celebrating the positive aspects of secularized culture means promoting those things that do not contradict the Christian revelation and the underlying values of Christian faith. Some examples of this adaptation include a clear celebration of what is good and beautiful and loving in the secularized cultures of the West. These are honest avenues that open up the Beauty, Truth, and Love that God is for all people. In the afterglow of the Enlightenment, secularized people search for small truths that can eventuate in the postulation of grand general theories.

As post-Enlightenment people, we must return to an evangelization that is holistic in attitude and approach. Evangelization has informational, pedagogical, experiential, psychological, physical, and social elements as well as spiritual ones. At its best, secularity serves to invite us into the present reality, to take hold of our lives, our communities, our societies, and our world, and to do something about it.

We are empowered to strengthen what serves the common good and to change what is harmful for the better. Redeeming the negative aspects of secularized culture means prophetic confrontation through dialogue and living Christian witness that risks serving as a countersign to the rationalizations of the present age. Seeking to be logical, practical, and realistic, we are called to redeem the utilitarian meaninglessness of this moment by reconnecting it with the transcendent perspective of the accumulation and culmination of all moments.

Just as secularism is the product of the slow turn of centuries, evangelical activity celebrating and confronting it must be a slow, patient, and gentle effort. However, some new elements are indicated. The future is not to be a replay of the past; the very mission itself has changed and with it the missionary must change. Most importantly, the bias of attention has shifted from an emphasis on a universal message by a universal church to include serious considerations of the local reality of the people for whom the mission of the church exists. It is not only "one Lord, one faith, one baptism" (Eph. 4:4–5) delivered from above to "save souls," but also many cultures, many languages, many experiences that must be accounted for in the sacramental exchange of a mutual evangelization in search of a universal sense of gospel truth. Laity, the vowed, and the ordained each have an important role to play in the mission in secularity, but not the same role, if the Second Vatican Council is taken seriously.

While the developing situation of secularization rushes along like a mighty torrent of cultural force, it might seem that we are merely treading water, swimming with halting strokes toward an adequate response. Risking the next steps into a committed direction could be a leap of faith toward new missionary effectiveness. It could also be a dive off the edge of a cliff into an abyss of confusion and self-doubt. The dangers, challenges, and opportunities of this situation are great. Therefore, they require an equal measure of careful and considered pastoral missionary reflection. Success may be measured in the short term and on the moderate scale, but ultimate success must be left in God's hands. Thus, while we struggle and thrash about, it is important to remember that there are strong arms and a steady grip to bear us up should we falter in our efforts. God never fails!

PART FOUR

A Note on the Symposia as Events and on Our Key Resource Persons

THE FOUR SYMPOSIA

THE 1998 General Chapter of the Missionary Oblates of Mary Immaculate had challenged its new General Council to work more deliberately on the question of what it can mean today to be a missionary within a secular culture. With this in mind, the General Council organized two initial symposia entitled "Missionaries to Secularity."

The first was hosted by St. Paul University, Ottawa, Ontario, and took place June 20–22, 2002; the second was hosted by Oblate School of Theology and the Oblate Renewal Center, San Antonio, Texas, and took place October 3–5, 2002. Each event, despite being invitational, attracted more than 150 persons. About half of the participants were Oblates, and about half were laypersons or other religious and priests. Both were events of communal prayer, communal search, high energy, intellectual stimulation, and warm fraternity. Both events too were international in character, drawing people from every continent, although, given the locale, the majority of participants were from North America.

On the strength of those two events, the Oblate School of Theology in San Antonio organized two further symposia: a large event that drew over two hundred people, held at the Oblate School of Theology in San Antonio, October 21–23, 2004. A smaller, think-tank, event took place in Toronto, Ontario, April 15–16, 2005.

The Ottawa Symposium, June 20–22, 2002

At the Ottawa event, our key resource persons were John Shea, a theologian-writer and storyteller from Chicago whose presentation was entitled "The New Dialogue with Secularity: Multidimensional Spiritual Living"; Richard Rohr, a Franciscan priest from the Center for Action and Contemplation in Albuquerque, New Mexico, whose presentation was entitled "Singing Songs of Sion in a Foreign Land"; Gilles Routhier, a professor of theology from Laval University in Quebec City, whose presentation was entitled "Risquer plonger en eau profonde: non plus seulement reamenager, mais retrouver les gestes des batisseurs"; Michael Downey, a theologian and writer who works full-time for the cardinal's office in Los Angeles and whose presentation was entitled "Theology's Prime Commandment: Understanding God's Kenosis"; and Vivian Labrie, who works full-time with and for the poor in Quebec City and reminded us of the place of the poor within missiology in her presentation, "Jeter les bases des sociétes sans pauvreté: Comment?"

We also invited a number of persons to lead focus sessions, namely, Maxime Chaigne, Edward Beck, Sandy Prather, Denis Paquin, Joanne Chafe, Bishop Jim Weisgerber, Normand Provencher, Chief Harry Lafond, Robert Michel, and Bishop Gerald Wiesner.

The First San Antonio Symposium, October 3–5, 2002

At our 2002 symposium in San Antonio our key resource persons were John Shea, who had also been with us in Ottawa and whose presentation was entitled "Gospel Stories: Resources for Contemporary Spiritual Living"; John O'Donohue, whose presentation was entitled "Poetics of Presencing: An Exploration of a Spiritual Landscape When the

Old Wells Run Dry"; Robert Schreiter, from Catholic Theological Union in Chicago, who clarified the landscape of secularity for us with his presentation, "Pathways to a New Evangelization in the First World"; Robert Barron, a young diocesan priest who teaches systematic theology at Our Lady of the Lake Seminary in Chicago, who brought the voice of a younger generation of Catholic thinkers with his presentation, "A Missiology of Aesthetics: The Icon of Jesus as a Paradigm"; and Mary Jo Leddy, who teaches theology and spirituality at Regis College in Toronto and is founder of Romero House, whose presentation was entitled "Naming the Present Moment: Culture, Spirituality, and Missiology."

Our focus sessions leaders were Marion Gil, Sandy Prather, Joanne Chafe, Wayne Holzt, Stuart Bate, Paul Fachet, and Ron Rolheiser.

The Second San Antonio Symposium, October 21–23, 2004

This symposium employed a different format wherein participants broke up into six streams of discussion: (1) "Ministry Inside of Parishes," led by Donna Ciangio; (2) "Ministry Outside of Parish Structures," led by Robert Schreiter; (3) "Preaching and Evangelization," led by Richard Rohr; (4) "Theology and Spirituality," led by Michael Downey; (5) "Ministering to Youth," led by Tom Rosica; and (6) "Vocations and the Renewal of Religious Life," led by Ron Rolheiser.

The leaders of each of these streams, along with John Allen and Walter Brueggemann, were our key resource persons. Ron Rolheiser gave a theme-setting presentation, "The Scope of Our Ecclesial Embrace: What Kind of Ecclesiology Best Undergirds Our Mission to Secularity?" to open the symposium; Walter Brueggemann gave the keynote address ("Nurturing Faith in a Secular Environment") the first evening; and each of the leaders of the various streams, along with John Allen, gave a presentation at the end of the symposium.

The Toronto Symposium, April 15–16, 2005

At our 2004 San Antonio symposium, a participant suggested that a next-step, follow-up to these symopsia would be for a small think-tank to gather, digest all the materials of the first three symposia, and within five to ten synthetic points formulate what we, on the basis of our conversations, want to say to a larger audience. Michael Downey, Robert Schreiter, Mary Jo Leddy, Gilles Routhier, Ron Young, and Ron Rolheiser were invited to do this.

They met in Toronto in April of 2005 and formulated what, in essence, is contained in chapters 2 and 3 of this book. Ron Rolheiser consented to be the editor who prepared the final formulation of this synthesis.

OUR RESOURCE PERSONS

O VERALL, we invited sixteen periti to play special roles at these symposia. In addition, we asked Reginald Bibby, who took part in smaller gathering in Edmonton in the summer of 2004, to submit an essay for this book. Ron Young, who took part in all four symposia, was also asked to submit a paper. The presentations of Robert Schreiter, Michael Downey, Mary Jo Leddy, Gilles Routhier, and Robert Barron are given in full in part 3 of this volume. Much of the substance contained in the other keynote presentations is woven into part 2 of this book.

The task here is to give a brief introduction to each of our major resource persons:

John Allen (Rome, Italy)

Rome correspondent for the *National Catholic Reporter*, John Allen authors a very popular Web site called *The Word from Rome*. He is also the author of a number of books, including *Opus Dei: An Objective Look behind the Myths and Reality of the Most Controversial Force in the Catholic Church* and *The Rise of Benedict XVI: The Inside Story of How the Pope Was Elected and Where He Will Take the Catholic Church*. We invited Allen on the hunch that a reporter for the *National Catholic Reporter* who has to work on a daily basis inside the Vatican would, because he has to bring together in his own life two rather different ecclesial visions, have something important to say to us.

In his address to us, he challenged us to be aware of our own non-listening, intolerance, and narrowness: Are we sufficiently aware and critical enough of how much secularity has shaped us? How much does ideology shape our criticism of the church? Do we exhibit the same incapacity for conversation with what's other to us as does secularity? Do we ever move toward those who are not like-minded?

Allen's comments at the end of the symposium are not fully recorded in this write-up, although they form part of the final mix, but some of his comments and reactions to the symposium can be found in *The Word from Rome* 4, no. 10 (October 29, 2004); *http://nationalcatholicreporter.org/word/*.

Robert Barron (Chicago, Illinois)

A diocesan priest from the Archdiocese of Chicago, who teaches at Our Lady of the Lake University, Barron is a gospel-artist and a gifted writer whose writings carry depth, color, passion, and commitment. He is deeply committed inside the community of faith. An academic, with a concern to renew the romantic imagination within Christianity, he is an apologist in the classic style of C. S. Lewis and G. K. Chesterton. He is also a mythical character in the occasional Andrew Greeley novel, where he is sought after by those who want to hear the opinion of "the young Father Barron!"

His challenge was strong and spoke for a new generation. He talked of the beauty of the Christian mystery, its unique depth, its stunning simplicity, and its wide comprehension. He then went on to say that, in his view, we should no longer continue to keep our faith private. Evangelization must show itself publicly, like it did in medieval pilgrimages and in today's World Youth Days. Faith must be expressed publicly, in colorful and romantic ways. We must, he insisted, "stop building beige churches."

Reginald Bibby (Lethbridge, Alberta)

Canada's best-known sociologist of religion and Board of Governors Research Chair in Sociology at the University of Lethbridge, Bibby has been studying religion in Canada for nearly thirty years and has authored eight best-selling books on religion, including *Fragmented Gods*, *Unknown Gods*, *Restless Gods*, and *Mosaic Madness*.

Addressing a satellite symposium in Edmonton, Alberta, Bibby stated: "The idea that people are turning away from religion hasn't held up. Canada continues to be an incredible Christian monopoly. Canadian churches, the established churches, continue to be in a good position. There is remarkable stability. God," he told us, "isn't in trouble just because many of us no longer go to church. God is never in trouble!"

Walter Brueggemann (Decatur, Georgia)

Well-known author and speaker and professor of Old Testament at Columbia Theological Seminary in Decatur, Georgia, Walter Brueggemann has been the recipient of many awards and honors, including seven honorary doctorates. He is best known in the larger community for his books on prophecy, imagination, and hope.

He was larger even than his persona. Looking very much like an ancient biblical prophet himself, he warned us of a double danger in dealing with secularity: losing ourselves within it, or, conversely, playing it too safe and creating little enclaves for ourselves. Secularity, he warned us, "can shrivel the human spirit" and "replace imagination with technology." Scripture, he assured us, gives us the tools to ground ourselves in a world beyond this one and to develop an alternative, prophetic imagination.

Donna Ciangio (New York, New York)

Head of the Pastoral Life Center for the U.S. Catholic bishops, Donna Ciangio has wide experience in facilitating groups, especially on the issue of ministry within parishes. It was that particular expertise upon which we hoped to draw.

In her presentation to us Ciangio spoke of the many challenges facing parishes today: the size of parishes, the struggle to give individual attention, lack of awareness of one's baptismal call, excessive individuality within the culture, constraints of time, different ecclesiologies, and generational differences within communities. She also spoke of larger tensions within the overall church: inclusion versus exclusion; empowering versus controlling; progress versus maintenance; and hierarchical approaches versus collaborative ones. She left us with a metaphor for leadership: Jesus washing his disciples' feet.

Michael Downey (Los Angeles, California)

A gifted academic and respected author, Michael Downey is the Cardinal's Theologian, Archdiocese of Los Angeles. An intellectual by nature and training, his major concern at this time is to build bridges between theology and spirituality in the most multicultural church in the United States.

He spoke to us on Christology, suggesting that a potentially fertile image of Christ for our secular culture might well be Christ as "the kenosis of God." Christ, in his self-emptying, expresses a love that gives itself and seeks nothing in return, incarnates God's presence without pretense, and reveals a God of total nonviolence and vulnerability, who is pure invitation and whose patience and understanding encompass even secularity.

Vivian Labrie (Quebec City, Quebec)

Widely known and respected in Quebec for her work with the poor and her attempt to take the gospel to the streets, Vivian

Labrie is articulate and prophetic. She speaks for the poor in the corridors of power, civil and ecclesial.

Her challenge was strong: Don't forget about the poor! The gospel is ultimately about God rescuing the poor, and part of evangelization must also be liberation of the poor. The church, she suggested, is a huge international body that potentially could do much more to alleviate poverty. Human solidarity, as much as dogmatic truth, she feels, is needed to move effectively against poverty.

Mary Jo Leddy (Toronto, Ontario)

Founder of Romero House (a house for refugees in Toronto), a co-founder of the *Catholic New Times* (an independent Catholic newspaper in Canada), and on the faculty at Regis College, Toronto, Mary Jo Leddy is many things: a respected spiritual writer, a theologian who has written with much insight about the cultural realities of North America, a Catholic journalist with a wide reputation, a popular teacher, and a woman who has sustained a long commitment to peace and justice. She has, in Canada at least, helped many Christians to maintain a joyous and prayerful commitment inside an institution, the church, even when they do not always agree with the direction the church is taking. She has modeled how to be prophetic and, at the same time, respectful, gentle, and gracious.

"We are better than we know and worse than we think," Leddy told us. Part of her message was that unless we regain our own inner vision and define ourselves more by what we are for than by what we are against, we will continue to divide from each other. What can offer us this inner vision? The Christian tradition offers that inner vision and throws light upon deeper realities, beyond the here and now, and, most importantly, it calls us to world citizenship, beyond our own backgrounds.

John O'Donohue (West Coast, Ireland)

Poet, writer, artist, scholar, John O'Donohue is a missionary to secularity. A scholar with a doctorate in philosophy (German Idealism), he, by choice, does not hold a formal academic post, but rather prefers to be an itinerant, popular scholar in the tradition of Erasmus.

His challenge was both strong and colorful: How does one become spiritual without leaving behind the physical, the emotional, the sexual, the bodily? To move beyond churches that are weary, gray, and tired, we must, O'Donohue suggests, move beyond clericalism, fear of the feminine, excessive fear of eros and a false reliance on authority and move toward reclaiming our mystical and intellectual traditions.

Richard Rohr (Albuquerque, New Mexico)

The founder and director of the Center for Action and Contemplation in Albuquerque, Richard Rohr is perhaps the most sought-after popular speaker in ecclesial circles in the English-speaking world. The author of more than a dozen books and dozens of series of audio and video cassettes, Rohr, in both his theology and language, models what it means to be a missionary within secularity.

Part of Rohr's message to us was his view that we are a faith community in exile — in exile from power, possessiveness, and the prestige we once enjoyed — and we need to remember that all transformation happens in exile because that is the only time that God can get through to us. Our task, he suggested, is to stay with the pain long enough until it changes us.

Ronald Rolheiser (San Antonio, Texas)

President of the Oblate School of Theology in San Antonio, Texas, Rolheiser has just finished a six-year term on the General Council of the Oblates of Mary Immaculate. He is the author of a number of books, including *The Holy Longing*, *The Restless Heart*, and *The Shattered Lantern*. He gave the opening theme-setting address at each of the symposia and acted as the general editor of this book.

Tom Rosica (Toronto, Ontario)

A Basilian priest who is at present director of Salt and Light, a communications ministry for the Canadian churches, John Rosica organized and headed up the World Youth Days when they were held in Toronto in 2002. Previous to that he served as chaplain at the University of Toronto. A close friend of John Paul II, he served as a television commentator for CBC television during the pope's funeral.

We chose Rosica to lead our stream on youth, not just on the strength of his having organized World Youth Days 2002, but especially on the strength of his work as chaplain at the University of Toronto, where he was able to build community across every ideological fault-line.

In his presentation to us, he challenged us to be more attentive to young people's desire for sacraments, scripture, and catechesis. He suggested too a biblical image that might be helpful to us in our work with youth: Jesus on the road to Emmaus. "Christ is incognito and walking along the road with us and, as at Emmaus, is asking us: 'Why are you so sad?'"

Gilles Routhier (Quebec City, Quebec)

Presently a professor of Religious Science at Laval University in Quebec City, Routhier is one of Canada's foremost ecclesial analysts. A gifted academic and a visionary, Gilles Routhier brings together good academics and a fertile imagination to envisage creative new ways in which the church might engage secularity.

Routhier suggested that perhaps we are asking our parishes to carry too many things, to do things that they can no longer do. Parish and mission, he submitted, are not coterminous, and we need to ask ourselves: Do we need new structures beyond and outside of parish that can better supplement what parishes can do? Can we dream of new "ecclesial houses"?

Robert Schreiter (Chicago, Illinois)

One of the major theoreticians of missiology, Robert Schreiter teaches and writes with a practical, artistic bent that makes him sought-after worldwide as a mentor in this field. We looked to him, among other things, precisely to keep us on the academic straight-and-narrow, should wildness and art have caused us to stray.

This he did, admirably, pointing out, among other things, that today's secularity has a particular set of characteristics: (1) it is an uneven terrain; (2) you cannot measure it simply by declining church attendance because there is still, inside of secularity, a strong, diffusive, belief in the supernatural, a believing without belonging; and (3) there is a resurgence of religious sensibility, carried by, among other things, our immigrant communities and the rise of various religious movements.

John Shea (Chicago, Illinois)

Former director of the Doctor of Ministries program at Mundelein, John Shea now works full-time in health care and as a writer. A respected academic theologian, presently engaged in writing a series of scripture commentaries, Shea might also be described as a gospel-artist, a storyteller, and a physician of the soul.

Among other things, he told us that recovering the tradition is a great labor and that we must seek to recover its core beyond its encrusted accretions and then put our own passion into that heart. Doing this, he submitted, will require of us a profound ascesis of listening. The cock will crow, Shea believes, when the ego cracks. There are, Shea says, many ways to wake up.

Ronald Young (Ottawa, Ontario)

An Oblate missionary with a Ph.D. in missiology at the Gregorian University in Rome, Ronald Young has taught missiology in San Antonio. More recently, he has moved to

St. Paul University in Ottawa to join its missiology department.

Young did not make a formal presentation at any of the symposia. His essay appears as chapter 11.

Also by Ronald Rolheiser

AGAINST AN INFINITE HORIZON
The Finger of God in Our Everyday Lives

Do you ever feel that your meditation is just a small corner of the divine in a difficult world? Best-selling author Ronald Rolheiser invites us to see meditation, and every aspect of life, as part of a world filled with God and brimming with possibility and hope.

Full of personal anecdotes, healing wisdom, and a fresh reflection on Scripture, *Against an Infinite Horizon* draws on the great traditions of parable and storytelling. In this prequel to the best seller *The Holy Longing*, Rolheiser's new fans will be delighted with further insights into the benefits of community, social justice, sexuality, mortality, and rediscovering the deep beauty and poetry of Christian spirituality.

"Ronald Rolheiser has mastered the old, old art of parable." — Morris West

"A felicitous blend of scriptural reflection, shrewd psychological observations, and generous portions of letters sent to Rolheiser and his responses." — *Commonweal*

0-8245-1965-5, $16.95 paperback

crossroad

Also by Ronald Rolheiser

THE SHATTERED LANTERN
Rediscovering a Felt Presence of God

The way back to a lively faith "is not a question of finding the right answers, but of living a certain way. The existence of God, like the air we breathe, need not be proven. . . . " Rolheiser shines new light on the contemplative path of Western Christianity and offers a dynamic way forward.

"Whenever I see Ron Rolheiser's name on a book, I know that it will be an amazing combination of true orthodoxy and revolutionary insight — and written in a clear and readable style. He knows the spiritual terrain like few others, and you will be profoundly illuminated by this lantern. Read and be astonished."
— Richard Rohr, O.F.M., Center for Action and Contemplation, Albuquerque, New Mexico

0-8245-1884-5, $14.95 paperback

Check your local bookstore for availability.
To order directly from the publisher,
please call 1-800-707-0670 for Customer Service
or visit our Web site at *www.cpcbooks.com.*
For catalog orders, please send your request to the address below.

THE CROSSROAD PUBLISHING COMPANY
16 Penn Plaza, Suite 1550
New York, NY 10001

All prices subject to change.

crossroad